PARISH NURSING:
THE DEVELOPING PRACTICE

Edited by

Phyllis Ann Solari-Twadell, R.N., B.S.N., M.P.A.

Anne Marie Djupe, R.N.C., B.S.N., M.A.

Mary Ann McDermott, R.N., M.S.N., Ed.D.

NATIONAL
PARISH NURSE
RESOURCE CENTER®

LUTHERAN GENERAL HEALTH CARE SYSTEM
PARK RIDGE, ILLINOIS

Library of Congress Catalog Card Number 90-62671

ISBN 0-9627625-0-4

Printed in the U.S.A.

Table of Contents

I. Parish Nursing: The Context for the Developing Practice

1. The Mission of Health and the Congregation
   L. James Wylie 11
2. A Historical Perspective: Wholistic Health and the Parish Nurse
   Granger Westberg 27
3. Society, the Parish and the Parish Nurse
   Judith Ryan 41

II. Parish Nursing: Models and Developing Practice Settings

4. Models of Parish Nursing: A Challenge in Design
   Phyllis Ann Solari-Twadell 57
5. The Developing Practice of the Parish Nurse:
   An Inner City Experience
   Jo Ann Gragnani Boss, Jennifer Corbett 77
6. The Developing Practice of the Parish Nurse:
   A Suburban Experience
   Susan Monaco 105
7. The Developing Practice of the Parish Nurse:
   A Rural Experience
   Jan Striepe 129
8. Adjustments, Myths and Realities of Parish Nursing
   Anne Marie Djupe 147

III. Parish Nursing: Issues and Concerns for the Developing Practice

9. Assessment: Yourself, the Congregation and the Community
   Anne Marie Djupe 161
10. Accountability: A Rationale for Documentation
    Mary Ann McDermott 181
11. Spiritual Caregiving: A Key Component of Parish Nursing
    Marcia Schnorr 201
12. Ministry to Ourselves and Others: Promoting the Balance
    Phyllis Ann Solari-Twadell 221
13. Curriculum Development for Parish Nursing:
    An Educator's Perspective
    Norma R. Small 235

IV. Parish Nursing: A Developing Collaborative Practice

14. Team Ministry in the Parish
    Leroy Joesten 251
15. A Perspective on the Physician's Role in the Developing
    Practice of Parish Nursing
    Greg Kirschner 267
16. Pastoral Reflections
    Gerald Nelson 277

Contributing Authors

Jo Ann Gragnani Boss, R.N., M.S.N., M.A.
Parish Nurse
Chicago Uptown Ministry
Chicago, Illinois

Jennifer Corbett, O.S.F., R.N., B.S.N., M.T.S.
Director of the Parish Nurse Program
Columbus-Cabrini Hospital
Chicago, Illinois

Anne Marie Djupe, R.N.C., B.S.N., M.A.
Director of Parish Nursing Services
Lutheran General Health Care System
Park Ridge, Illinois

Leroy B. Joesten, B.A., M.Div.
Director of Parish Relations
Lutheran General Hospital
Park Ridge, Illinois

Greg K. Kirschner, M.D., M.P.H.
Associate Director
Lutheran General Hospital
Family Practice Residency
Park Ridge, Illinois

Mary Ann McDermott, R.N., M.S.N., Ed.D.
Associate Professor
Maternal Child Health Nursing
Niehoff School of Nursing
Loyola University
Chicago, Illinois

Susan Monaco, R.N., B.S.
Parish Nurse
Visitation Church
Elmhurst, Illinois

Gerald W. Nelson, B.A., M.Div.
Senior Pastor
Our Savior's Lutheran Church
Naperville, Illinois

Judith A. Ryan, R.N., Ph.D.
Vice President: Aging Services
Congregational Health Services and Health Policy
Lutheran General Health Care System
Park Ridge, Illinois

Marcia A. Schnorr, R.N., Ed.D.
Nurse Educator
Kishwaukee College
Malta, Illinois

Norma Small, C.R.N.P., Ph.D.
Director of Graduate Nursing Programs
School of Nursing
Georgetown University
Washington, D.C.

Phyllis Ann Solari-Twadell, R.N., B.S.N., M.P.A.
Director of Congregational Health Partnership
Lutheran General Health Care System
Park Ridge, Illinois

Jan Striepe, R.N., M.S.
Project Manager
Parish Nurse Project
Northwest Aging Association
Spencer, Iowa

Granger Westberg, D.D.
Consultant
The National Parish Nurse Resource Center
Park Ridge, Illinois

L. James Wylie, B.A., B.Th.
Senior Vice President
Corporate Church Relations
Lutheran General Health Care System
Park Ridge, Illinois

PREFACE

*T*his book represents the work of many who have been pioneers in developing the concept and role of the parish nurse. The editors have worked to identify the context for the developing practice, the models and the emerging practice settings, as well as the issues and concerns relevant to this collaborative practice.

Each author brings experience and expertise in defining and relating aspects of parish nursing as it is today. It is our purpose to bring together some of the concepts which form the basis for this type of ministry as well as to give the reader a better understanding of the various dimensions of the role. We have also included reflections from persons of various disciplines who work closely with the parish nurse and have supported them in developing their role.

We recognize that the concept is not new. Deaconesses and other religious men and women worked as part of the early church nurturing health and healing. However, it is only in the last five to six years that the idea of a parish nurse serving as a member of the church staff has been implemented. In spite of this short time, much has been accomplished across the country. Today, parish nurses can be found ecumenically from coast to coast.

This developing practice has a great potential for providing primary preventive health care services as well as assisting people to access the health care system. Parish nursing also provides a concrete way for churches to play an instrumental role in promoting health, healing and wholeness to the members of the congregations and community.

The book has been divided into four sections. Section I: The Context for the Developing Practice describes the historical as well as current trends in religion and health care which have set the stage for creative and collaborative ways to address the health care crisis in America today. Section II: Models and Developing Practice Settings describes the experience of the parish nurses along with some of their joys and frustrations in a new role and setting. Section III: Issues and Concerns for the Developing Practice seeks to describe some of the unique aspects of nursing which surface in this role. Section IV: A Developing Collaborative Practice includes reflections and perspectives from two key partners, the physician and pastor.

Although this text consistently uses the terms ''congregation,'' ''parish'' and ''church'' to describe a faith community, or the building in which the faith community worship, the intention is to be ecumenical in perspective. ''Mosque,'' ''temple,'' ''synagogue'' or other affiliated terms could all be used interchangeably throughout the text.

We have utilized the pronoun ''she'' when referring to the parish nurse. For male parish nurses, please accept our apologies. We value and support your participation and contribution to this developing role.

There are a number of acknowledgments to be made. The editors first of all wish to thank Rev. Granger Westberg for his pioneering spirit and leadership, for his teachings on the relationship of faith and health, and for recognizing the special gifts and talents of nurses. We also wish to thank George B. Caldwell, former President and Chief Executive

Officer of Lutheran General Health Care System, for his initial acknowledgment and investment in the program, and to Stephen L. Ummel, current President and Chief Executive Officer, for his continued support. We would like to acknowledge the consistent administrative support given to the Lutheran General Hospital Parish Nurse Program since its inception. We thank Rev. L. James Wylie for keeping the vision alive and Rev. Lawrence Holst for implementing the program. We thank Dr. Judith Ryan for her administrative support and encouragement. We would also like to acknowledge the contribution made by each author and our gratitude for their willingness to share their knowledge and experience. We are especially grateful to Karen Cornforth for her unlimited patience and gracious spirit in typing the manuscript and meeting deadlines as well as her dedication to the concept. We are grateful for the recent addition of our new secretary Bethany Johnson and for the gifts that she brings.

There are also some individual acknowledgments to be made. Ann Solari-Twadell thanks her mother, Phyllis H. Solari and her daughter Kimberly Ann Zych — two women who have taught her about love and caring for another. She is grateful to her husband Stephen for his understanding, patience and support, and her stepson Eric for the sharing of his life with her. In addition, she would like to acknowledge the gracious direction provided by John S. Klein and the Rev. John Keller. Individually, she is grateful for the teaching and guidance provided by the Rev. L. James Wylie. Her contribution to this work is dedicated to her deceased father, Archie J. Solari.

Anne Marie Djupe thanks her husband David and her son Paul for their continued love and support. She expresses gratitude to her parents, Rev. Walter and Esther Johnson, who live and model a life of caring ministry. When she first heard Granger Westberg speak 18 years ago, he described the kind of nursing ministry in which she believed. She feels privileged to have worked in a Wholistic Health Center and then with the parish nurse program at Lutheran General Hospital (LGH). She thanks the LGH faculty, Rev. Lawrence Holst, Rev. Lee Joesten, Chaplain Florence Smithe, and Dr. Greg Kirschner, for their collegiality and encouragement and all of the LGH parish nurses, past and present.

Mary Ann McDermott thanks her husband Dennis and her children, Dennis, Michael, Sarah and William, for facilitating her interest in the parish nurse role. Thanks to her dean, Dr. Julia Lane and her colleagues at Loyola University School of Nursing, particularly Ida Androwich and Mary Lynch who were essential in the initial development of the program at St. Ignatius Parish and to the faculty, students, pastors and parishioners who have continued to make the program flourish. She has been delighted to have been affiliated with the Lutheran General Health Care System as a member of the system and hospital governance and as a member of the previous Advisory Committee of the National Parish Nurse Resource Center.

Finally, we are grateful to God for all parish nurses, past and present, who have pioneered in this role and whose story is a part of this book.

Ann Solari-Twadell
Anne Marie Djupe
Mary Ann McDermott

FOREWORD

*U*nfortunately, most readers of this book will be nurses and pastors.

Now that I have your attention, given that crabby opening line, let me say what I mean by that opening word "unfortunately." Certainly it does not imply lack of respect for members of the nursing and clergy professions. They are key to the development of the parish nurse concept and to realizing it. And — now let me use the second person — you nurses and nursing educators, you ministers and priests who have this book before your eyes, may not represent a congregation of the "converted." Which means that the authors of this book do not assume they are only "preaching to the converted."

You may be only half-converted. That is, if you are a nurse, you are almost certain to be tantalized by the vision of parish nursing offered here, but you may immediately lose heart when you picture how hard it is to realize the role. Again, you may be only half-converted as a pastor because, while you will see at once where this concept fits into the theology and mission of a congregation, you may have a hard time summoning energies to add "one more thing" to the complex institution to which you minister in the name of Jesus Christ. Your table and agenda are full.

Yet, I am convinced in both cases that you will be convinced by the arguments, inspired by the vision, and informed by the practical details of this book. The worry is that neither you nurses nor you pastors, without whose support the parish nurse project will get nowhere, will be lonely, apparently self-interested promoters. "Unfortunately," you cannot carry it by yourself. Now let me drop the second-person language and start talking also to other readers who, one hopes, might be looking over your shoulder or might respect your recommendation.

Fortunately, for example, this is a book for finance committees and stewardship committees of congregations. Pastor Granger Westberg, in his lucid and memorable account of how the parish nurse program was invented, tells how he worked his way around congregations, making the case. All went well until he reached the finance committee. There the trouble started. How can an item costing $10,000 or more be fit into a congregational budget? In his story, they are not villains but realists. Some of his best friends, and mine and yours, are no doubt on finance and stewardship committees, or should be. They simply know how hard it is to get busy congregations and their members to give priority to something new.

One could say that the parish nurse program is a great money-saver, but that does not work well, because most members will never know it. A young politician doing some apprentice or intern work for a United States Senator once told me of his work on a piece of legislation. As I recall it, the law would simply seek to enforce the demand that freight trains come equipped with a certain kind of flashing strobe light which would serve as a warning to cars approaching crossings. From studies made in the states which enforced and did not enforce such laws, it was estimated that about 20 lives would be saved every year. "Unfortunately, those 20 people will not ever know that this law, and the action by this senator, saved their lives, but, still, their lives will be saved."

There is no doubt, no doubt at all, that a parish nurse will similarly save people money. They help teach "preventive medicine," which is the least expensive form of care there is. Through their counseling, their referrals, their "brokering" and "fixing," there is no doubt that they will help individuals, insuring agencies and governments save money in a time of a health care financing crisis. One could verge on the point of overselling by reminding that healthy congregants are more free to give more woman-hours and man-hours through their congregations to the service of others, and that the parish nurse program will help keep more of them healthy. But I use the fiscal theme here at the beginning only to symbolize the fact that there are large potential audiences for this book and to express the hope that it reaches them.

Why make such a fuss about the locale for this recently developed form of service? Why focus on the congregation, when, historically, people have connected through the nursing profession with hospitals, "visiting," or home care — but not with places that have steeples and domes, altars and high steps which made things hard for people in wheelchairs? Why?

Some years ago while writing about health and medicine in our part of the Christian tradition, I interviewed the presiding bishop of a denomination in that tradition. What advice could he give to someone who has just been given medical bad news? His answer: "My advice is that that person should have been an active member of a vital congregation for quite a few years." Meaning? Meaning that when misfortune comes, it is important to be part of a community of care. A congregation enfolds one in intercessory prayer — loving one's neighbor on one's knees. A good congregation provides care and casseroles, rides to clinics and cards for the bedside table. It represents a gathering of people who have heard and keep on hearing the word of the Healer, who are busy interpreting the message of wholeness in a world of brokenness. By their own stumbling words, halting actions, and only sometimes distracted thoughts, they help the person who is ill come to terms with some of their problems, to cope, and, in a way to transcend them on the pilgrimage to triumph.

So: the congregation is important. It will become more so as people realize its vital role in a time when health care in traditional institutions is simply beyond the range of more and more people, in a time when expenses grow. Not too long ago, a veteran physician who cares for aged people told me that he visited his 90-year old father daily in a Jewish senior citizens' home. This physician can afford the best of care, and provides it, for a man whose dignity is threatened along with his memory, which fails him thanks to a disease. "I have to say," said this Jewish physician, "that for all the professionals in his range, the person who treats my father as a dignified and worthy human being, and who seems to get some response, is a young black aide who probably will tell you she does that for him because she loves Jesus." The doctor went on to use that as an illustration of a resource in the believing community. "You folks spend too much time working on the religious angle in hair-raising, urgent, sudden health care crises — like "shall we pull the plug? Religion has most to offer in terms of long-term care, of sustained relations, where year in and year out people have to be motivated to take care." Congregations exist for that, and the parish nurse program helps them realize such care intelligently.

In a way, the invention of the parish nurse concept is part of several revolutions going on before our eyes, but hard to define and grasp.

First, it is part of a revolution in understandings of health and medicine. For two centuries we had been moving, usually unwittingly but sometimes wittingly, into accepting the model — the jargon has it "paradigm" — which saw that only conventional science could cure. Invest enough in research, make enough discoveries, develop enough professionals, build enough institutions, spend enough money, show enough awe, and such science would take care of our problems.

Today that model or paradigm is very much in question, not least of all among many scientists, researchers, discoverers, professionals, institution-builders and appropriators. They are coming to recognize that humans have or are "healing systems" which come into positive effect only when they are seen in the context of the larger systems around them. Westberg reminds us that the parish nurse program was nurtured by a hospital which believes in human ecology. Believing thus, it promotes the idea that we humans have to be seen in the delicate web and fibers of our contexts which include God, nature, others and the self.

Of course, the search for a new paradigm can lead to many devices or prescriptions which can delude and misuse people. Some uses of the term "wholistic," for instance, are connected to ideas which connect the individual to the universe, its forces and energies, in such a way that the individual is "part of God" or "becomes God," or is offered complete transcendence of suffering and care. Often this goes by the code word "New Age" holistic care. Without needing to contend that nothing good comes from disciplines connected with such an approach, we can observe its limits. People do keep suffering, falling ill, and dying in spite of their beliefs of that sort — or, for that matter, their belief in the God beyond the gods who is the Creator, the Healer, the One who cares and weeps with us on the path to fulfillment.

The parish nurse concept is born in an entirely different context of "wholistic" care. It knows that in congregations people hear messages, and try to realize them; messages directed to a world in which hate and misery, limits and pain, doubt and despair threaten almost as much as love and joy, boundary-breaking and pleasure, faith and hope are promised and realized.

Not many seasons ago, I presented an essay by a Christian neurosurgeon to a secular group of physicians, humanists and social scientists. He told what the service of "Christ crucified" meant to him when he interpreted his vocation, his life in respect to patients. Of course, the author reminded readers, he stayed within the bounds of his profession, and kept the physician's covenant that one keeps in a pluralist society. That is, while he may use "invasive" techniques in brain surgery, he is not "invasive" in respect to patients' belief systems, not disruptive of their patterns, not ready to be distracted from what they have sought by coming to him. It was a nice, important distinction, without which he could not function and help in healing.

One of the participants in the group spoke up in response. I suppose a stereotyper would call him a latter-day Marxist social scientist. That is, he uses Marxist techniques of social analysis to call into question the professions and structures of our society. (He does have a good mind, and does not offer Marxian therapy, simply "socialized" care, at this late date.) But he spoke up for others in the group when he said he hoped that the surgeon was not engaging in a new version of the body-mind distinction. That is, when this Christian deals with the body, he is nothing but a scientist and when he deals with the mind, his mind, he is a believer. Without spelling out how, this professor said he hoped that the physician was more "wholistic." He should use his faith to engage in critical analysis of how his profession works and through what institutions he works and toward what end they are all directed.

This is not the place to follow up on what all that means and can mean. It is the place to remind ourselves that, in even the most apparently remote corners of "scientific" and "academic" life, thoughtful people are giving second thoughts to the place of faith in the provision of health care. It may take a few minutes to work such people around to understanding the vital role of congregations in the ecology of the lives of half of America. It may take a few hours to help them come to see the promise of the parish nurse program in respect to that role. This book will certainly help in such tasks.

Most readers, however, are not going to be Marxist sociologists, scientific skeptics, secularists whose spiritual imaginations have atrophied if they were ever given a spiritual vision at all. Most readers will be nurses and pastors, church committees and, one hopes, theologians, people whose own imaginations may have been atrophied or whose vision has not yet been caught. They are people for whom constraints of time and money will be in the front of the mind, but in whose hearts the Holy Spirit, who "calls, gathers, and enlightens" the congregation is also active.

One of the great advantages of parish nurse work, in contrast to that of the neurosurgeon in a high-tech hospital or the employee in a tax-supported institution, is that nurses work in a context where certain meanings are allowed to be developed explicitly. Theologian James Fowler has written on the two languages of pluralist society. On one level, out of respect for each other, in a spirit of tolerance and deference, to keep civil peace, we do not always "unload" the whole focused theme of our beliefs. Often we may feel that those beliefs could be of direct aid to someone else. Still, the rules of the game call for some holding back. For example, one doesn't enter into an interfaith dialogue and then suddenly change the rules of the game midway and try to pounce on partners with pitches for conversion.

At the same time, says Fowler (I am rephrasing a bit), sometimes this situation makes us feel as if we are biting our tongues, choking to hold back what we might utter, holding our breaths, or stepping cautiously because we know there is a particular story, a special language of faith, a distinctive grasp of God's grace, which would be of greater aid than the language we would elsewhere use.

The parish nurse program works chiefly in congregations or communities where a certain language of faith is ready at hand. This does not mean that the nurse becomes preacher, has to be an explicit teacher, or a theological expert. It means that she or he knows that the Christian story is privileged and not only can be brought up, but is expected to have its place. It means that the nurse works in an ecology of meanings and care which encourage the drawing on that message of grace and the practices and habits it encourages.

One of the rules of etiquette for writers of forewords to books is that they should not give the plot away. There were many times as I read this manuscript when I wanted to steal more than the single Westberg story of his encounters with finance committees, in order to lure readers on. But these authors can and do speak for themselves. One of my marginal notes on the manuscript of a practical essay in this book — and there are several — is "these authors think of everything." This is "how to" literature of a high order. Maybe what makes it all hold together is that it is also "why to" literature. We have needed that and will need it if we accept the "risk" about which Westberg speaks and dreams. We might risk helping discover and invent something new in human care at a time of great need, when hearts grow faint but the message of God in Christ does not.

Martin E. Marty

Martin E. Marty is the Fairfax M. Cone Distinguished Service Professor at the University of Chicago, Senior Editor of The Christian Century and Senior Scholar-in-Residence (and editor of Second Opinion) at the Park Ridge Center for the Study of Health, Faith and Ethics.

Section I

PARISH NURSING:
THE CONTEXT FOR THE DEVELOPING PRACTICE

1

THE MISSION OF HEALTH AND THE CONGREGATION

L. James Wylie

*T*he ministry of health is central to the congregation. Stated another way, the congregation's central mission is that of "restoration." The Christian Church, indeed the entire community of faith globally, has no more important mission than health and healing. This chapter will focus on referencing theological foundations for the health and healing mission in the congregation, a historical overview of the congregation as a health and healing place, and current changes along with prospects for the 90's.

Theological Reflections

One could assert that God has been about the healing or restoration of His creation from the beginning. As illustrated in the Genesis narrative, it has been the teaching of the Church that, early on, the intentions of His creation were abridged by the willfulness of humankind in various activities which are generally categorized with the simple everyday word "sin." It is the view of faith that the problems of the world in one way or another are traceable to the collective determination of human beings throughout history to willfully rebel and/or deviate from the purposes of God.

It has been the understanding of the Hebrew world and the Christian era that all healing or restoration is from

God and indeed is integral to His ongoing participation in creation. The actions of human beings facilitate healing. God, however, is the source of all healing.

It is the teaching of the Church, as represented by all three ecumenical creeds where creation is focused upon in the First Article, that God created in the beginning. Creation is wholistic and interrelated in nature. The terms we ascribe to health and salvation are from the same Hebrew language root words (Richardson, 1956). In recent times, many understand salvation to be primarily spiritual in nature.

From the perspective of our faith, the Kingdom of God is in the process of being revealed and experienced as God's creation is being healed. The work of Jesus Christ and the ministry which He initiated and we follow, is intended as a model and an example of the way in which the faithful are to proceed as the agents of God in bringing restoration to a fallen creation. We recognize that this Kingdom will not fully come and this restoration will not fully occur during our lifetime; and in fact, it will not fully occur until the end of time. The scriptures say, "in the fullness of time" there will be the signaling of the end of the age. The faithful will be called to His right hand to inherit the Kingdom "prepared for you from the foundation of the world." The self-centered rejecters of His saving grace will be directed toward the left, that existence prepared for the self-willed rebellious crowd typically referred to in the scriptures as "Satan and his followers."

It is important for us to understand some basic terminology. Until recent times "wholism" was reserved for students of cosmology; but now it is becoming part of the common language. The term has significant recognition if not understanding. In the roots of our faith the Hebrew term "shalom" encompasses the perspective of wholeness which is "the desired intent of creation." It implies the activities and behaviors which best maintain and promote the development of a peaceful, that is, balanced, understanding of existence. Further, it suggests the relational nature of all things — the balanced, symbiotic dimensions of the created order (Richardson, 1956, p. 165).

All of this we understand and confess when we recite the creeds and confessions as part of our worship setting. Typically, we do not carry the full understanding and concept with us in the recitation of the English, but it is important to lift up this understanding here because it becomes the foundation for the healing ministry. Healing, properly understood, does not guarantee a return to a prior living status, but has more to do with a fullness or completeness of the human experience. It is important to emphasize that it is not limited to physical welfare; indeed, some healed persons live with chronic physical conditions.

Historical Perspectives

The ancient Greeks and Romans perceived healing and religion as identical. Temples were used as the site of sacrifices to soothe the anger of a god or seek favor so that health could be restored. Temples were known as places of healing. The Greeks' domination by the Romans brought the knowledge of healing into the Roman culture.

Healing is prevalent in the gospels. Jesus was very focused on the health of people. This is known to be true because he performed more miracles of healing than of any other category (Scherzer, 1984). Jesus acknowledged the scientific information available during his time; however, he did not stop there. He put great emphasis on the importance of psychological and spiritual factors in sickness and health. He stressed the interrelationship between all the factors of a total person. In some instances, psychological or spiritual factors were noted as the cause of the physical disorder (Luke 5:18-36).

Most of us are prepared to acknowledge and accept the fact that the congregation's mission is shaped by the ministry that Christ initiated. We refer back to Christ's dusty trips with his band of twelve as the beginning of the Christian community. Paul, Peter and their associates set about establishing congregations, or more accurately in many cases, seeking to bring the messianic understanding to existing Hebrew communities of faith.

If those early congregations had had a mission statement, it would have included three elements: 1) to teach and preach, 2) to conduct worship and promote fellowship, and 3) to perform service — direct service such as healing the sick, feeding the hungry and providing comfort and protection to the widows.

As this review continues, one element which is of significance is that of the diaconate. Deacons and deaconesses carried the church into people's homes. It is important to note that the nursing profession traces its beginnings to these early Christian orders. It was the deaconess Fabiola who founded the first charity hospital in Rome about 300 A.D.

During the medieval age, the Church was the primary vehicle through which the healing arts were promulgated. Through this entire period, monks and some sisters were engaged in the work of healing. It was not uncommon for monasteries and convents to have rooms for the sick. Hospitals were built in connection with some churches (Scherzer, 1984).

The Crusades, although not accomplishing their primary purpose of regaining the Holy Land, did have an influence on the Church and health. Leprosy was an illness brought back to Europe from the Orient. As it spread, the Church tried to respond. Hospitals were built, and were called "lazarettos" after Lazarus the Leper in the New

Testament. During one period, there were 2,000 lazarettos in France and 200 in England (Scherzer, 1984). This highlights the effect of the Crusades, the institutionalization of health care, the building of hospitals, the need for increased religious nursing orders, and a renewed interest in healing.

Continuing with this overview, two events appear to have influenced the estrangement of the Church and formalized medicine. The emperor Constantine not only legitimatized Christianity, he went on to take the "service" component of the congregation's life and assign it directly to the bishops for their development and supervision. Therein, the direct ministries of health and restoration were essentially removed from the congregation (Wietzke, 1987).

It is one of those things of which it might be said, "seemed like a good idea at the time." Indeed, the purpose was to bring sustaining stewardship to the service components lest they go astray at the changing whims of a congregation. One might even make the case that he had sufficient insight to understand that these components are best not carried on by the government as such, but by the faith sector. At about that time the Church organization as such, under the bishops, became directly involved in supervising the service component of the congregation's activity as a function of the bishop's office. Over time, this changed the role of a specific congregation and began the institutionalization of these services. In later centuries in Europe, and to a lesser degree in America, especially Protestant groups and congregations moved out on their own through what were called "mission societies" doing "service" at home and abroad as an expression of their personal faith, independent from the work of bishops and formal church structures.

A second major influence, not directly associated with the Church, fueled the separation of the Church further from developing medical science. The influence of the philosopher

Descartes in the mid-1600's emphasized the dualism of spirit and body. This dualistic construct had been brewing in the culture, including the faith community, for a number of years. This view of man came to be pervasive, if not characteristic, of western civilization. This division has persisted until modern time.

Starr (1982), in the text The Social Transformation of American Medicine, gives a compelling and revealing perspective in the titling of the first book, "A Sovereign Profession, The Rise of Medical Authority and the Shaping of the Medical System." This book describes the impact of economic and conceptual forces which edged the Church from its center stage position to stage left. It found particular expression in America with the development of the medical health establishment over the last 75 to 80 years, with the clergy and their associates supposedly pursuing the matters of the spirit while physicians and their associates in medicine supposedly pursuing the matters of the body. In more recent times, the emotional specialists ended up primarily in the medical dimension but with certain representations in the spiritual community as well.

After World War II, with the onset of specialization within medical development, a reconciliation between clergy and physicians and these two worlds of spirit and body began to surface. The mid-century contribution of physicists moved us from a Newtonian understanding of the universe to a wholistic cosmology, an understanding of all elements of the universe as having a basic synergy and interrelationship. In these movements and with the powerful popular application of private individuals, we have the beginnings of this current time, an era of renewed emphasis and acceptance of wholism.

As noted previously, in the earliest of times typically the spiritual and physical agent of healing was the same person; indeed, this phenomenon persists in many world cultures to this day. However, in the western culture these roles were separated, and health concerns became medicalized and separated from salvation concerns in the mindset of most people. Within the last 40 years, the term "health" has become a synonym for the "medical world." Today when we use the term "health care," we are often referring to services provided by physicians or agencies or hospitals, recognizing as we do, that these services are in almost every instance focused on caring for persons who are struggling with disease. Our institutions spend little time on health promotion. Very little emphasis was placed upon health in our culture until the early 50's when the "wholistic" terminology began to be revived through insightful leaders such as Dr. Granger Westberg and Dr. Frederic Norstad (Norstad, 1968). In recent years, the wholistic emphasis has continued and is usually the terminology of choice for the conceptual framework of health care. More recently, the term has shifted to include health promotion and wellness activities, both from the point of view of their effectiveness and from the perspective of attempting to reduce expenses associated with remediation and treatment.

The importance of this understanding for us is that it gives the rationale and foundation for efforts to reestablish the congregation as the primary focus for health, not medicine or treatment. This becomes a key element in a social strategy to bring about a new way of thinking and behaving.

It is also important to have firmly in mind the "birthright" which we have, one to which parish nursing brings primary instrumentation. Our birthright declares the congregation as the chief and primary focus for health and salvation. When one uses those words together in the English they slide down fairly easily. But when one drops the word "salvation" and then says, as is the title of this chapter, that the primary ministry of the congregation is a health ministry, that often catches in the throat. If you are not already there in your thinking, you need to be invited to radically focus in this direction.

Nurses, as well as others, need to be well grounded in this understanding both theologically and historically. One of the reasons to be knowledgeable on this subject is that you will need to interpret it to a congregation that has been raised on an understanding that health is the property of the medical community. This thinking needs to be changed. Health is the property of, or better the responsibility of, each of us. When we have refocused the congregation and the community of faith on its primary role, we are then able to properly position the role of the hospital, the physician and other service providers as partners in the health enterprise. We then understand the need for active engagement with our Creator in the process of reclaiming and healing His creation. From this perspective, no matter how complicated it seems or how sophisticated we have become in talking about this in academic and scientific circles, the premise is very simple. This has not been in good perspective in our time and emphasizes the need to be about changing our thinking. In other words, all need to develop a proper "mindset," particularly the members of the community of faith (Wylie, 1987).

To help us further understand this opportunity in history, I bring to mind the picture which Dr. Granger Westberg has brought to us in what he calls "The Double Wedge: The Three Acts of Illness" (Peterson, 1982). Although some of the particulars of his presentation may not reflect the delivery of health care today, to me it is one of the simplest yet most profound assessments of what has happened in health care in the last 40 to 50 years.

His account goes like this:

> Often functional illness is described as developing like a dramatic production, a play in three acts. The

'technical' name for what goes on in Act I is 'little-bit-sick.' The name for Act II is 'sicker,' and the title for Act III is 'really sick.'

In Act I, you are cruising along through life working hard, attending daily to the stream of obligations and joys with which you surround yourself, and somehow you begin to notice a nagging sense that everything is not right. The first person to notice that you are sick is you. You suddenly realize that you don't feel so good. You're a little-bit sick.

Then you begin to try to figure out what's going on for you. You act as your own doctor, listen to the symptoms, and make a diagnosis. You may decide that the cause of the problem is that you've been burning the candle at both ends and not getting enough sleep. Your fatigue and headache are the first signs that you've noticed that you're not getting away with this pace unscathed. So you decide on a treatment. 'Every night for the next five nights, I'm going to bed at ten o'clock, then I'll see what happens.' You treat yourself. If your diagnosis was accurate, based on your knowledge of yourself, and if you do follow your treatment plan, then probably you get well again.

Most of us do this all the time. We go in and out of Act I continually, constantly adjusting our schedule, pace, and ways of taking care of ourselves in light of the feedback our own systems provide us.

But, let's say you don't listen to yourself and your feedback, and you keep pressing on and working too hard. You may get sicker. Then next you begin to notice that something's wrong in your family. One of them says, "Hey, Dad, is something wrong? You don't look well and you've sure been a grouch." And you reply, "No, nothing's wrong. I am not irritable. I AM NOT IRRITABLE!" But, if you listen to the feedback of your family, acting as your doctor, you may decide to change your pace, and get yourself well again.

You discover that you're in Act II of illness when you come to the realization that you are sick enough that you need to do something about it right now. So you decide to call your family physician and see him as soon as possible. You go to see him the same afternoon. Let's say he's the listening kind and he listens to your problem. Then he examines you, and together you sit down and talk . . . and he says, "You know, Joe, I really think your fatigue and headaches are related to the stress you're under. Now what can we do to help you make some changes in your life-style?"

If you listen to him, and the two of you decide on ways to lessen the strain on you, then you probably move back out of Act II, through Act I, and get well again.

If the treatment you and your doctor decide on doesn't work, or if you don't follow his advice, you may go back three or four times for the same problem. Finally, he may say, "Well, Joe, I think you'd better come into the hospital for a checkup."

So, you go into the community hospital for your checkup, which may include x-rays, extensive laboratory work, perhaps even exploratory surgery. Then another diagnosis and treatment plan are made and you get well again.

Many people go through a large portion of life seldom getting sicker than this. Thus, the family physician can take care of almost all health problems you experience throughout life.

A small percentage of us get sicker than Act II, and move into Act III. The family physician finally doesn't know what to try next. He feels he can't handle the problem any longer and he says, "I would like you to see a friend of mine who is a specialist."

Now you see the specialist. He focuses on the problem; and, of course by now your problem is pretty big. We need to be careful not to be critical of the family doctor who couldn't define the problem fully, since he saw you when it was much smaller. The specialist is able to recognize and deal with your problem because it's big now, and because he knows this particular type of problem very well. Occasionally, he says, "You know, I think you'd better come to the hospital." So you go to the research and teaching hospital, and there you see not just specialists but a super-specialist, or sub-specialist.

The specialists and sub-specialists on your case put their collective heads together and do some remarkable work with your disease, and you get sent back to your family doctor, and then to your friends and family, and you get well again.

At the far end of Act III looms Act IV, the realm of undertakers and ministers. Most of us spend our lives trying to stay out of this Act.

Approximately 60 percent of the sick people in America in any one day are in Act I. They are doing all kinds of things to take care of themselves: home remedies, sleep, exercise, and rest. In Act I, however, we have approximately 3 percent of the doctors — those in epidemiology and preventive medicine.

When you move to Act II, we find roughly 30 percent of the sick people and approximately the same percentage of doctors. These are generalists, family practice physicians, internists, and pediatricians. Finally, when you move into Act III, there are approximately 10 percent of the sick people, but approximately 70 percent of the doctors.

The general trend for movement of professionals is into earlier stages of illness and prevention, rather than cure. Many specialists would love to see people earlier in Act II instead of Act III. Many general family practice physicians are talking more of prevention today. They would love to be in Act I rather than Act II. For years there have been few physicians interested in Act I. The revolution that's beginning to take place in medicine is characterized by a renewed interest in prevention, and a desire to move care back into earlier stages of illness.

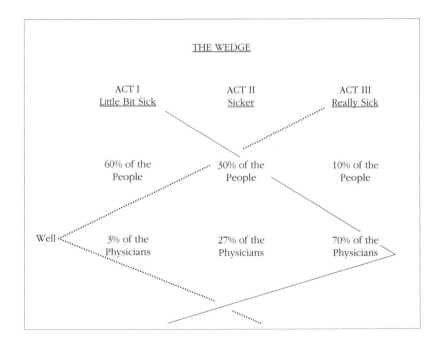

It is not necessary for a huge percentage of physicians to suddenly start working in Act I. This involvement would not efficiently utilize the high level technical training of physicians. It is necessary, however, to take seriously the educators, clergy, counselors, nurse practitioners, and others with expertise and interest in the preventive efforts necessary for assisting persons in the first act of illness — before they get sicker.

"Act I" is the primary arena for the parish. It is, of course, where most of the people in America are; they are not patients in hospitals or chronic patients in doctor's offices.

A further analysis of this model as to the distribution of resources and emphasis in our culture will suggest why Westberg's analysis is so profound. While most of the people are in "Act I" where a little health promotion/disease prevention might well keep them out of "Act II," the primary emphasis and dollar commitment in this country is in the technology of "Act III," with a major investment in the medical business in "Act II." Society is attempting to deal with this disparity through the efforts of government, business and private groups. The time is ripe for all sectors of society to pull together to address all three acts in a more cohesive and cost-effective manner.

This is a very exciting time to refocus on the congregation as a "health place." Some denominations, institutions and congregations are already beginning to address this issue.

Since 1986, Lutheran General Health Care System has been involved in an effort called Congregational Health Partnership. In 1988, The Evangelical Lutheran Church in America (ELCA) became a partner in the work, the primary focus of which has been to develop a new "mindset" among members so that they see their congregation as the starting point and sustaining point in matters of health and healing (Solari-Twadell, 1987).

The Chicago Metropolitan Synod of ELCA has begun an emphasis on "Health and Healing for Church and Community," which seeks to understand the activities of the Synod as carried on in the context of health and healing as portrayed in this chapter (Hicks, 1990). Nationally, the American Protestant Health Association and the Catholic Health Association are focusing efforts on getting their hospital members to form new relationships with congregations and faith communities.

Of equal significance is the prospective opportunities for the health care picture in America. The fact is that in spite of America's success, it is in the throes of a health policy struggle the likes of which we have never seen. Driven by concerns about cost, we have come inevitably to the point of questions relating to quality and appropriateness of care along with concerns about access and distribution. The hi-tech forces are not in phase with hi-touch. The corporate re-structuring of provider organizations characteristic of the 80's has wound down and the words heard more than any other across the realm are "quality" — "total quality management" — "continuous quality improvement," and this in an industry that for years has prided itself on quality. The Joint Commission on Accreditation of Healthcare Organizations (JCAHO) and prestigious medical leadership in this country join in the observation that quality is not documented nor reliably available in America. It is in this arena that the Church seeks to make entry. I say entry, for although many an institution bears its name, few retain a sense of faith accountability.

In all of this, the Church is pondering what to do, and in some cases seeking to get involved through political advocacy. At the same time, the medical community is beginning to refocus on the spiritual dimension in caring and curing. It is a time of immense change and rethinking. In the final analysis, the Church needs to be there out of its own need as well as for the good of society. The congregation needs to play a more dominant role in this new beginning. The point is that a congregation which has a clear perspective and program with regard to its health ministry, totally integrated with its activities of worship, fellowship, teaching and preaching, is a very ready component for the social transformation that is needed in health care.

Financially, there is a need to address more of the needs of people in "Act I" of illness; further, there is a need to properly allocate our technical capabilities in "Act III". It is my impression that many physicians think that institutions could do better in terms of resource allocation in "Act II" as well. The opportunity at the congregational level is to form partnerships with the players in "Acts II" and "III" and primarily to get a firm grip on the opportunities which the Church has in "Act I." Unique opportunities exist at the parish level that go beyond diagnosis and triaging and focus on a wide range of services, cradle to grave, in regard to health promotion and opportunities for service.

The central mission of the congregation is health and salvation; and in so saying, properly understood, I have said one thing, not two.

Reference List

Hicks, S. (1990). Health and healing for the church and community. Initiative of the Metropolitan Chicago Synod. Unpublished manuscript. Chicago, IL.

Norstad, F. (1968). Human Ecology. Medical Ecology and Clinical Research. 7(1). Park Ridge, IL.

Peterson, W.M. (Ed.). (1982). Granger Westberg verbatim. Hinsdale, IL: Westberg Institute.

Richardson, A. (Ed.). (1956). A theological work book of the Bible. New York: The Macmillan Company.

Scherzer, C. (1984). The church and healing. Unpublished manuscript, Deaconess Hospital, Evansville, IN.

Solari-Twadell, A. (1987). Congregational Health Partnership. Chronicle of Pastoral Care. 7(1) Park Ridge, IL.

Starr, P. (1982). The social transformation of American medicine. New York: Basic Books, Inc.

Wietzke, W.A. (1987). A Premium Congregational Health Partnership. Congregational Health Partnership.

Wylie, L.J. (1987). Primacy franchise for health: The parish. Chronicle of Pastoral Care. 7(1) Park Ridge, IL.

2

A HISTORICAL PERSPECTIVE: WHOLISTIC HEALTH AND THE PARISH NURSE

Granger Westberg

*I*t all happened quite spontaneously. A group of us had been experimenting since the late 60's with wholistic health centers which were family doctors' offices in churches. Our aim was to see if we could bring about whole-person health care in a church setting by having spiritually oriented family doctors, nurses and clergy working together.

It was a project enthusiastically sponsored by the W.K. Kellogg Foundation and the Department of Preventive Medicine and Community Health of the University of Illinois College of Medicine. More than a dozen of these medical clinics were begun in neighborhood churches in upper, middle and lower income areas in cities around the country (Tubesing, 1977; The Wholistic Health Centers: A New Direction in Health Care, 1977; Wholistic Health Centers: Survey Research Report, 1976).

The evaluations of these doctors' offices in churches over a period of ten years indicated that the quality of care offered when these three professions worked together under the same roof was measurably more wholistic than the average doctor's office. Further, it was clear that the nurses in each of these centers were the glue that bound these three professions together in a common appreciation of the healing talents of each.

The evaluators, being disinterested scholars coming from nonreligious backgrounds, began with a bias against the possibility of scientific medicine and religion actually collaborating in a joint approach to the problems of individual patients. Over the years, they saw that it was working very well. As they tried to ascertain why it worked, they gradually came to the conclusion that most of the nurses employed in these clinics could speak two languages: the language of science and the language of religion. The nurses were acting as translators. They helped the doctor and the minister communicate in ways that were helpful to a "whole person" approach to health care.

As inflation swept America and it became more and more expensive to start new wholistic health centers in churches, someone said, "If the nurses in these clinics have proved so valuable, why not try placing a nurse on the staff of a congregation and see what happens?" When we asked individual nurses about this idea, the response was so immediately favorable we decided to try it.

I went to Lutheran General Hospital (LGH) because I have had a longstanding relationship with several of the founding leaders of the hospital. Lutheran General Hospital, located in a northwest suburb of Chicago, Park Ridge, Illinois, showed immediate interest in participating in a pilot project. This hospital of 713 beds had long given leadership in the pastoral care of its patients. The hospital, founded in 1959, has described its philosophy as "a human service organization committed to the philosophy of Human Ecology. Human Ecology is the understanding and care of human beings as whole persons in light of their relationships to God, themselves, their families, and the society in which they live." Currently, some 25 chaplains work closely with physicians, nurses, social workers and many other health professionals in an unusually effective team approach.

An administrative team from Lutheran General Hospital was organized to plan and implement the first institutionally based program. I was asked to go out and meet with pastors and congregational members. We were seeking to have six churches initially participate in the program. We also decided to go to large churches of various denominations which might be able to afford hiring a nurse. Initially, we were asking the church to pay the full half-time salary of about $10,000.

As I met with the pastors and described the concept, about 75% showed great interest and 25% some interest. They readily recognized that the nurse would be a person to assist them in their ministry to people who were hurting, and many whom they felt they could not adequately serve by themselves.

I then asked the pastor if there was a group of people that I could talk to some evening and describe the concept. In many cases, the group consisted of nurses and other health professionals from the congregation. The response was immediately positive. The next group I was invited to speak to was a decisionmaking board such as the church council. I described the overall picture of health and the role of a nurse in the church. Again, the response was very positive.

All responses were positive until I met with the finance committee. They immediately began to express concerns about their budget, and finding the resources to support another position. Many felt they could not fit the position into their current budget. Each of the churches I talked to had good reason for their financial concerns. Many were involved in building or renovation projects. It was then that I realized something very important. None of these large churches had a line in their budget with funds appropriated for "risk taking." Consequently, I had to go elsewhere to find funds. So I went back to the hospital and explained that none of the churches, regardless of size, were willing to risk the salary of $10,000. This was 1984.

With the help of Lutheran General Hospital administrators who were eager to respond to the churches' willingness to participate in such a program, a plan was developed. LGH agreed to pay 75% of the salary the first year while the church would pay 25% to begin. It was decided that the second year, the church would increase their contribution to 50%, 75% the third year, and full payment by the fourth year.

With the new proposal that they would contribute 25% of the salary the first year, six churches were willing to participate and agreed to a three-year trial period. Four of these churches were Protestant and two were Roman Catholic. They were located as close as six blocks away from the hospital and as far as 30 miles away.

In early 1985, the hiring process was begun. An advertisement in a local paper brought some 30 applications for these half-time parish nurse positions. The quality of the candidates was deemed to be amazingly high as interviewers from both the hospital and the churches discovered hidden talents in these nurses. By and large, they were women (no male nurses applied) in their thirties and forties whose smaller children were now in school. They all showed genuine interest in a type of nursing which would allow the kind of creativity they had always longed for.

All of the candidates were stimulated by the potential of a whole-person approach to their work with people. The fact that they would be working within the context of a congregation and actually serving on the pastoral staff of that church was of great interest to them. Most of the candidates indicated that their original motivation for going into nursing was strongly influenced by a desire to incorporate the spiritual dimension into their work.

After choosing six nurses to participate in the program, we decided not to superimpose upon them a course of instruction because we were not at all sure the direction such a course should take. Instead, we invited them to spend a half day each week at the hospital in an informal discussion group where, in the presence of a teaching chaplain, a nurse educator and a family practice physician, they could describe what they felt they needed in an ongoing educational process.

Once a week, the nurses came to the hospital for three hours. We began each day by going around the circle of six parish nurses and asking them to tell of their experiences in the parish during the preceding week. In the early weeks, it took anywhere from an hour to an hour and a half for these women to tell the stories of their ministry. The telling of these stories brought about all sorts of questions, spontaneous role-playing of situations, even tears and laughter, as everybody took part. At the end of every session, we were all exhausted, but also exhilarated to think that these unusual happenings were taking place simply because a nurse had been added to the staff of a church.

The parish nurses told us of their many opportunities to talk with people informally between services, at coffee hours, at meetings of church organizations, at pot-luck suppers and in home visits with the sick or shut-ins. It was in the informality of it all that we saw the nurse having the unusual opportunity to talk with people in the early stages of illness. Before these people ever thought of going to see a doctor about their very minor problems, the nurse, with her unique sensitivity to early cries for help, was already responding to it.

It gradually dawned on us that churches are actually the one organization in our society most suited to give leadership to the field of preventive medicine. Scientific medicine has not been known for its contributions to preventive medicine. Jeff Goldsmith, national health care advisor, says that the nation's health care system still acts as if most diseases strike "like a fire in your house," rather than "like a fire in a pile of leaves." And, as a result, he says health care is preoccupied with climbing ladders and chopping holes in roofs instead of keeping a bucket of water and a rake nearby.

The history of the parish nurse movement is closely tied up with an understanding that churches, when they are functioning at their best, are dedicated to keeping people well. This means tending the little fires in piles of leaves. But most people do not see churches and synagogues as an integral part of our present health system (Westberg, 1988). If a pollster asks the question, "What are the health agencies in your community?" the usual reply speaks of local hospitals, and perhaps, a well-known medical clinic.

When we speak of health care, we usually mean "sickness care." And that's where hospitals and doctors' clinics do such a good job. So, we still have to raise the question, "What are the institutions of our culture that keep us well?" There are at least five, offhand — the home, the school, the church, the workplace and the public health department. We are well aware of the sickness that follows when any of these five is not doing its share toward building in a quality of life that builds up immunity to disease.

The churches and synagogues of America are becoming self conscious of their role in keeping people healthy. They have never really seen themselves as part of the nation's health system, because health had to do with a complex thing called "medical technology," which was becoming more technical every day. Almost with the same suddenness, society is realizing that many illnesses are preventable.

Most illnesses come on slowly. It is as if our bodies were trying to tell us something — something about how our way of looking at life, or our way of handling life's many problems, is making us sick. At least it is making us more vulnerable to the germs attacking us. If a great deal of illness is related to our way of looking at life — our outlook on life, our philosophy of life — then, of course, religious institutions must be integrated into the health care system.

It is precisely at this point that parish nurses are seen to be natural organizers of congregations as community-based health centers. Almost two thirds of the people in the United States have some tangible relationship to congregations. Churches of all sizes and shapes are to be found in all corners of America. And in almost every church there is a registered nurse. Many large churches have 25 or more nurses in their membership. But most of these churches have never even thought to use these nurses in any creative manner, until recently.

During the first year or two of the parish nurse project, it became clear that there were five areas of ministry in which the nurses were engaged. These will be described later in this volume, but let me just mention them here:

1. The parish nurse is a health educator.

2. The parish nurse is a personal health counselor.

3. The parish nurse is a coordinator of volunteers.

4. The parish nurse helps people relate to the complex medical care system.

5. The parish nurse assists people to integrate faith and health.

Actually, what these five areas describe is what the parish nurses attempt to do by engaging the entire congregation in seminars, workshops, Sunday forums, etc., where they can all grapple with the concept that true health includes the spirit. It is not all physical or nutritional.

Sixty years ago, a best-selling book by the famous missionary to India, E. Stanley Jones, entitled The Way (Association Press), contained the following quotations which help us understand that the Christian Way provides an excellent foundation for healthful living.

> When we live the Christian way, we are living the way we were made to live . . . made in the inner structure of our being.
>
> Evil is a turning of the natural into the unnatural — it is a living against life.
>
> Self-love, the natural, can become selfishness, the unnatural.
>
> Self-respect, the natural, may be lured into pride, the unnatural.
>
> Love, the natural, can be beguiled into lust, the unnatural.
>
> Sex desire, the natural, can be lured away from its God-intended creative function and become an end in itself.
>
> These simple, natural functions, dedicated to God and controlled by God bring life — life to the whole person. But if they become god, become ends in themselves, there is one result, death; death to development, to happiness, to the whole person. (Jones, 1930)

E. Stanley Jones and many other Christian divines through the centuries were remarkably aware of the whole-ness concept which many of us are coming to see as a sensi-ble approach to health. It gives validity to the entrance of churches into the health field.

Many active, dedicated church members of all branch-es of Christendom are searching for ways to make the mes-sage of the Christian faith more relevant to our age. They are fascinated by the way Jesus in his healing ministry always dealt with people as whole persons. They are disturbed that our present highly technical health care system tends to neglect the spiritual dimensions of illness. Just as the ecologi-cal movement has captured the imagination of youth throughout the world, so now it is just possible that the whole-person emphasis in health care will be included in those splendid concerns.

Many churches want to make a more meaningful con-tribution to society. They feel that they are stagnating be-cause they spend so much of their time just talking. They want to become involved in action that leads to a healthier society. It is time to bring religiously oriented people into the discussion of what is meant by high-level wellness. If we can agree on a number of major religious concepts — stated clear-ly and succinctly — concerning what we believe "health" to be all about, then our chances of getting church people and health care people to work together on joint projects will in-crease greatly.

Let me suggest nine statements which possibly could be accepted by a wide variety of religious people.

    1. "Health is intimately related to how a person 'thinketh in one's heart.'

2. Physical health is not to be "our chief end in this life," — only a possible by-product of loving God and one's neighbor as oneself.

3. Health is closely tied up with goals, meaning, and purposeful living: it is a religious quest, whereas illness may be related to a life that is empty, bored, without purpose or aim.

4. Our present disease-oriented medical care system must be revised to include a strong accent on modeling and teaching prevention and wellness.

5. Our present separation of body and spirit must go, and an integrated, wholistic approach put in its place.

6. There is a difference between merely existing and a life lived under God, responsive to the promptings of God's spirit.

7. The body functions at its best when a person, who is the body, exhibits attitudes of hope, faith, love and gratitude.

8. True health is closely associated with creativity by which we as people of God participate with God in the ongoing process of creation.

9. The self-preservation instincts of the human can be happily blended with the innate longing to love and to help others." (Westberg, 1982)

We who have been engaged in the parish nurse movement have found much meaning and challenge in the widespread determination to understand the meaning of the word "health" as much broader and deeper than ever before. It is a natural part of the vocabulary of the Bible and of Christian theology. "And thy health shall spring forth," is a famous quotation from Isaiah. "Health" and "salvation" are words used interchangeably throughout the Scriptures. Parish nurses are engaged in doing the Lord's work when they assist in encouraging people to move toward the whole-person goals of the highest scriptural injunctions.

Parish nurses are now serving in hundreds of churches throughout the country, united in their desire to bring "salvation to people," understanding that the basic meaning of the word "salvation" is "being made whole." The Great Physician knows that not everyone wants to be made whole. The Church is in the motivation business. It understands how important it is to motivate people to want to live healthier lives. Christ himself asked that question of the man at the pool of Bethesda: "Do you want to be made whole?"

The whole-person movement takes a person's belief system seriously. If one's belief system is faulty, it affects the way the body functions. If wholistic concepts can be integrated with one's religious beliefs, then each will provide motivation for the other.

This is a time in history when the Church is sorely needed to help motivate people to put body, mind and spirit together and to convince them that the integration of these three can lead to truth, health and wholeness.

Let us sum up some of our reasons for believing that churches provide a natural setting where parish nurses can do their most effective work as health educators, health counselors, coordinators of volunteers, agents of referral into our complex medical system and integrators of faith and health.

1. Churches are to be found everywhere, out in neighborhoods where people live — urban, suburban, rural — and their buildings are largely unused during the weekdays.

2. Churches have a long history of serving their communities through social activities and continuing education programs.

3. Churches symbolize our need to take seriously the problems of the human spirit which are so often related to the causes of illness.

4. Churches provide a remarkable reservoir of dedicated people who are willing to volunteer their services to assist in humanitarian endeavors.

5. Church members have a growing appreciation for the opportunity to model, in their own church buildings, the need for cooperation between scientific medicine and religious faith.

The role of parish nurses is basically a reaching out for more whole-person ways of ministering to people who are hurting. There is a slowly growing desire among many health care professionals to integrate human caring with the achievements of hi-tech medical care. Most of them are under such restraints of time and bottom-line concerns they cannot practice what they know would be better health care.

Parish nurses have the unique opportunity of demonstrating effective ways of combining the strengths of such collaboration between the humanities and the sciences.

Reference List

Jones, E. S. (1930). The Way. New York: Association Press.

Medical Ecology and Clinical Research. (1968). 1(1), Summer. Lutheran General Hospital, Park Ridge, IL.

Tubesing, D. (1977). An idea in evolution. History of the Wholistic Health Centers Project 1970-1976. (1977). Society for Wholistic Medicine, 137 S. Garfield, Hinsdale, IL.

Westberg, G. (1982). The Church as Health Place. Dialog. 27(3) pp 189-191.

Westberg, G. (1988). Parishes, nurses and health care. Lutheran Partners. Nov/Dec. pp 26-29.

Peterson, W.M. (Ed.). (1982). Granger Westberg verbatim. Hinsdale, IL.: Westberg Institute.

The Wholistic Health Centers: A New Direction in Health Care. (1977). Experience report for W.K. Kellogg Foundation, Battle Creek, MI.

Wholistic Health Centers: Survey Research Report. (1976) Wholistic Health Centers, Inc. Society for Wholistic Medicine, 137 S. Garfield, Hinsdale, IL.

3

SOCIETY, THE PARISH
AND THE PARISH NURSE

Judith A. Ryan

*L*utheran General Health Care System (LGHCS), an institution of the Evangelical Lutheran Church in America (ELCA), is a national network of caring institutions that strives to represent the healing ministry of the Church throughout the United States and in Sweden. For 30 years, this health ministry has been seated within Lutheran General Hospital in Park Ridge, Illinois. In more recent years, the System launched Parkside Medical Services Corporation to provide a national system for care of persons suffering from alcohol and substance abuse and other addictive behaviors. In 1985, LGHCS restructured its efforts to provide options for older adults and established Parkside Senior Services, a national network of older adult services.

LGHCS has also worked closely with the church at large through three unique programs: the Park Ridge Center, the Parish Nurse Program and Congregational Health Partnership.

The Park Ridge Center
For Health, Faith and Ethics

In partnership with the former American Lutheran Church, the System created and endowed the Park Ridge Center for the study of ethical issues related to health, faith and ethics. The Center's Project Ten series of books, the quarterly Second Opinion and regular publication of the Park Ridge Bulletin all contribute to the understanding of bioethical issues from the religious dimension.

The Parish Nurse Program

Since 1984, LGHCS has established parish nurse programs in 30 congregations. These nurses are engaged in a wide variety of health risk assessment, Christian health education, health promotion and primary and secondary preventive services. The system's sponsorship of the National Parish Nurse Resource Center was initiated in 1986. The Center serves as reference center for information about the philosophy and work of nurses in parish nurse programs; as a convener of annual educational programs on parish nurse developments; and as consultant to other denominations and religiously affiliated health care systems on organizing parish nurse programs.

Congregational Health Partnership

In 1986, a new program was initiated with the ELCA: The Congregational Health Partnership (CHP). CHP is a conceptual framework which has as its goal to promote a mindset amongst members of a faith community to see their congregation as a health place. This effort seeks to strengthen relationships between and among members of the congregation, between and among congregations themselves, and between and among the congregation, the church at large, church-related health care institutions and the communities we all serve. The partnership involves LGHCS, the ELCA Divisions for Congregational Life and Social Ministry Organizations, and seven congregations.

The Need

Why? Why are the Church, a large tertiary care facility, and local congregations investing hundreds of thousands of dollars and volunteer hours in the concept of Congregational Health Partnership? Because we believe that the mission of the congregation, the Church and the religiously affiliated health care system is unique, and that if we are to express a Christian mission of service, we must together address the major structural shifts going on in the society around us.

The insatiable demand for drugs, dramatic escalation of crime and homicide among our children, and the prevalence of AIDS all speak to a breakdown in very basic human relationships, family structures, sources of authority and underlying values.

The aging of America has introduced a new and costly burden of care. Our very capacity to use medical technology to save those at high risk has raised new questions of burden of care and quality of life. The simultaneous increase in infant mortality and increasing number of infants and children among the homeless has raised new questions of intergenerational equity. Even those most advantaged among us express a sense of brokenness and loss. Roles are no longer simple. The very basic roles of man and woman have shifted . . . as have those of father and daughter, mother and son. The average children of today will spend more time caring for their parents than their own children.

The Problem

The problem is that no one organized sector of our society is prepared to manage this massive change. The failure of the Church, the public sector, the private sector, the not-for-profit sector, and the consumer sector to perform their historic roles in health, healing and wholeness has been publicly documented. Furthermore, the health services sector itself is increasingly broken.

The Historic Church

In the first 300 years in the life of the Church, certain key elements contributed to congregational vitality, even under conditions of persecution (Wietzke, 1987). Teaching, preaching, worship, fellowship and service were interwoven in all activities of the Church. The results were magnificent. "Christians," said pagan adversaries, "have turned the world upside down." In the fourth century, Emperor Constantine entered into an alliance with the Church in order to secure political control of the growing organism. In this fateful union between church and state, one of Constantine's most significant moves was to place service concerns under the Office of the Bishop. These concerns encompassed care of the poor, hospitality to strangers, and other forms of service meant to enhance the expression of Christian love. Ironically, Constantine's move, removed service concerns from normal congregational life.

The modern Church, subsequently, was bequeathed only "two-thirds of the pie." The legacy stemming from Constantine's action emphasizes only preaching, teaching, worship and fellowship. While American Christianity supports a variety of service enterprises, it does so out of a stewardship commitment, supporting global mission activities, hospitals, metropolitan ministries, and so on and so on. But increasingly, the means by which service is offered are apart from — separate from — external to — normal congregational life. And even in this area, current data would suggest while some 40% of health care services in this country used to be supported by the Church and other philanthropic institutions within society, after the advent of Medicare and Medicaid and state intervention in the financing of health programs, that portion of revenue has dropped to less than 2% (Bernardin, 1988).

The survey of caregivers recently conducted by the American Association of Retired Persons demonstrates that the Church is not perceived to be a source of essential support or services (AARP, 1989).

The Four Social Sectors

The four primary sectors of society that have historically dealt with society's obligation for health and human service are the public sector, the private sector, the not-for-profit sector and, more generally, the consumer sector.

The public sector is generally defined to be the governmental sector. Faced with a deficit the interest on which alone absorbs nearly 20% of our gross national budget, and with an aging population entitled to unprecedented benefits, the reaction of the governmental sector has been to say, "Read my lips. There will be no new entitlement programs."

The private sector is generally defined to be the business or corporate or employer sector. Faced very directly with the challenge to compete in a global economy with a retired work force which, including employee dependents, is now larger than that of its active work force, the strategy of the private sector has been set. The message of American business related to health benefits is clear: "Shift the cost to the user." As a result of this strategy, we see employers negotiating back benefits, we see an increase in the number of employees of small corporations who are uninsured or underserved, we see managed care systems growing, and we see an escalation in the number of occupationally based health promotion and prevention programs. But the underlying strategy is not health, it is cost control.

The consumer sector perceives the crisis in health care to be one of fragmentation and of out-of-pocket cost. This was perhaps best demonstrated in the political fiasco related to catastrophic coverage, in which the elderly population of this country either believed that they could not afford any more out-of-pocket costs for health care or were somehow so estranged when the new catastrophic coverage was not designed to cover the catastrophic costs of long term care, that they forcefully rejected the need for additional dollars to cover the catastrophic costs of acute medical care. At any rate, "No More Out-of-Pocket Costs" is the political message that they very effectively delivered to the Congress of the United States.

The Fragmentation of the Health Care System Itself

There are three major fragmented sectors of the health care system itself — one focusing on acute care, one focusing on long-term care, and one at least attempting to focus on primary care. These three sectors are governed by very separate social policies, the financing mechanisms that drive each of them are separate from one another and they are structured in a very insular manner separate one from the other. The caregivers struggling to meet escalating demands are isolated within each of these sectors.

The acute care model is illness based, characterized by high technology and highly specialized providers, by episodic reimbursement, by hierarchy of decision making, and is individual patient centered.

Acute Care Model

- Medical Diagnosis (Illness Based)
- High Technology
- High Specialized Providers
- Rigid Professional Boundaries
- Episodic Reimbursement
- Acute-Care Institution Based
- High Occupancy/Specialized Units
- Patient-Centered/Resource Intensive Model
- Hierarchy of Decision Making (Appeals to Authority)
- Power of Protected Information
- Crisis Management
- Individual Patient/Disease Outcome Oriented

The chronic care model is based on functional outcomes, is characterized by low technology, by generalist providers, and by case reimbursement.

Chronic Care Model

- Functional Assessment (Deficit Based)
- Low Technology
- Generalist Providers
- Softer Boundaries Between Professions
- Case-Based Reimbursement
- Long-Term Care Institution Based

- Declining Occupancy/Swing Beds
- Cost-Containment Model
- Multidisciplinary Consultation (Collaborative Decision Making)
- Power in Shared Information
- Strategic Management
- Aggregate Functional/Outcome Oriented

The primary health care model is focused not only on the health of the individual patient, but on the health of family and surrounding community. It relies more on the informal caregiver, and is characterized by prospective or capitated or managed care payment mechanisms.

Primary Health Care Model

- Health Assessment (Attribute Based)
- Self-Managed Technology
- Primary Care Providers
- Integration of Professional Providers with Informal Care Givers
- Prospective/Capitation Payment Systems
- Commuity Based

- Home Rather Than Institutionally Based
- Prevent Cost Model
- Shared Decision Making (With Client and Family/Community Systems)
- Power in Patient/Family/Education/Information
- Long-Range Planning
- Community Health Status Oriented

Because no one sector can by itself effect fundamental change in the health care system in this country, it seems imperative that some creative combination of the four be constituted. Together they could build a unique system for enabling universal and equitable access to a full range of essential primary health care, long-term care and acute medical care services in the United States.

Oneness In Purpose

What does all this have to do with the parish nurses? What unique contribution can our churches and church-related health care institutions make to resolving the problem which none of the very broad sectors of society — including the health care system itself — seem to be able to address?

A major American growth area over the past 10 to 20 years is not even recorded in the economic figures: the "Third Sector," comprising nonprofit, nongovernmental community services, both national and local, secular and religious. Local "pastoral" churches, Protestant and Catholic, evangelical and mainstream, that focus on the needs and concerns of their individual members, particularly those of the baby-boom generation, are growing even faster than the large national nonprofit organizations. There are now at least 10,000 such churches with memberships of 2,000 or more, twice the number of such churches 10 years ago (Drucker, 1989). Furthermore, it has been estimated that more than 65% of this nation's citizens identify in one way or another with some kind of faith community.

We would therefore propose that the Church at large, working in partnership with its health care agencies and institutions, can make a very practical difference.

First, the Church can act as a refuge or community alternative to our liberal culture (Marty, 1990). The liberal culture, the environment in which contemporary medicine, research and most care is carried out is characterized by commitment to skeptical reason, enthusiasm for tolerance in lifestyle and social norms, and affirmation of the central importance of the individual and individual freedom.

"The Faith Community in America has and continues to provide alternatives where liberalism is unsatisfying. We turn to congregation (or synagogue or mosque or other holy place) as refuge from this culture, not merely for escape but as when an army retreats to prepare for other encounters. And in faith centered gatherings contemporaries go on to find or build the community which the individualist culture largely fails to provide." (Marty, 1990)

Second, the Church, through its tradition and theology, serves to build communities of values, offering sustaining interpretations, healing sets of meanings, symbol, sacrament and liturgy that help the individual to experience the healing presence of Jesus Christ (Marty, 1990).

Third, the healing tradition is or can be embodied in the action of faith communities, which provide intercession, casseroles, parish nurses, adult forums, support groups, healing services, pastoral counseling, befrienders, shelter for the homeless, and a variety of congregationally based primary health promotion, prevention and maintenance services where the liberal (secular) culture often runs out of resources or patience (Marty, 1990).

On October 25-27, 1989, the Carter Center of Emory University and the Wheatridge Foundation convened heads of the major faith communities in the United States to address the following goal:

"To seek new ways to more fully involve the church in building healthy lives for all people by reducing unnecessary suffering, preventing disease, disability, and premature death, and improving the quality of life."

This conference was a follow-up to the initial symposia convened by the Carter Center in 1984 to define the causes of premature death in the United States and to suggest intervention strategies. Those precursors were defined to be:

-Alcohol Dependence & Abuse
-Arthritis & Musculoskeletal Diseases
-Cancer
-Cardiovascular Disease
-Dental Disease
-Depression
-Diabetes Mellitus
-Digestive Diseases
-Drug Dependence and Abuse
-Infant Mortality/Morbidity
-Respiratory Diseases
-Socioeconomic Status
-Unintended Pregnancy
-Unintentional Injuries
-Violence: Homicide, Assault, Suicide

Because each of these precursors has behavioral components, it was the conclusion of those assembled at the Carter Center in 1984 that the Church provided the unique social structure through which corrective behaviors might be molded.

The Carter Center Conference in 1989, therefore, called on all faith communities to seek new ways to prevent disease, disability and premature death and to improve the quality of life by reducing the gap between what is known about disease prevention and health promotion and the application of that information.

The Carter Center chose to showcase the parish nurse as the one professional through which the church might help to address the gap between what we know about health and what we do about it.

The Parish Nurse

The philosophy of parish nursing is to promote the health of a faith community (churches and synagogues) by working with the pastor and staff to integrate the theological, psychological, sociological and physiological perspectives of health and healing into the word, sacrament and service of the congregation. The parish nurse focuses on the clinical application of health promotion concepts specific to adults and families. As a member of the ministry team, the parish nurse is a qualified health care professional who can work with parishioners to resolve concerns such as interpersonal relationships, grief, guilt, stress, lifestyle, life changes, spiritual resources and outlook on life, all of which are known to affect the health status of individuals and families. He or she is a practitioner prepared to assess the needs of the whole person — psychological, physical, sociological and spiritual. The nurse facilitates positive lifestyle changes through health assessment, counseling, self-help groups, health education, and referrals to other health care providers and community resources.

What difference would investment in the parish nurse make to broader societal problems? First of all, we would propose that one purpose of the parish nurse is to give expression to the concept of service within the congregation. By rendering very practical service, by providing concrete care for the individual's physical, emotional and spiritual health, and by helping to integrate concepts of health into the teaching, preaching, stewardship and fellowship mission of the Church, the parish nurse makes a very concrete contribution toward the reintegration of the concept of service into the mission of the modern church.

Second, we would propose that the purpose of the parish nurse is to actualize the idea of the church as a caring community, as an integrator across sectors of society.

By assessing the parishioner's need and referring that individual and family to sources of medical care, pastoral counseling, long-term care, Medicare and Medicaid, the parish nurse is making concrete the integrative role of the Church across sectors of society. Furthermore, by building bridges across congregations, between congregations and health providers, and among congregations and community organizations, the parish nurse is helping to assure that the Church will be at the table as an acknowledged participant in the debate and decisions about how and what kind of health care services should be provided in this country.

And finally, we would propose that the parish nurse can give expression to, or demonstrate the idea, that primary health care services can be integrated into the present mission of religiously affiliated health care institutions. By doing this, the congregation and related health care institutions can together make a real contribution to the reintegration of health care services across the acute care, chronic care and primary health care sectors.

Conclusion

The parish nurse is a unique professional response to the health care crisis in this country. By providing a congregationally based source of primary preventive and restorative care, addressing both the health and faith dimension, linking that role to community-based and inpatient centers with the capacity to address both physical and spiritual needs, religiously affiliated health care systems could make a significant difference to the community's health and well being, rebuild a sense of congregational 'ownership' of religiously affiliated hospitals and other health-related institutions and agencies of the Church, return the congregation to its central place in the community as proclaimer of the Word, administrator of sacrament, advocate, servant and health place, and help this nation to heal.

Reference List

American Association of Retired Persons. (1989). National Survey of Caregivers: Summary of Findings. Washington, D.C.: Author.

Drucker, P. F. (1989). The nonprofits quiet revolution. Leadership, Tenth Anniversary Issue.

Marty, M. E. (1990). Theology and the tradition of the church in health and healing. Second Opinion, 13. Chicago, IL: The Park Ridge Center.

The consistent ethic: An interview with Joseph Cardinal Bernardin. Joseph Cardinal Bernardin. (1988). Second Opinion, 8. Chicago, IL: The Park Ridge Center.

Wietzke, W. A. (1987). A Precis on Congregational Health Partnership. Park Ridge, IL: Lutheran General Health Care System, Congregational Health Partnership.

Section II

PARISH NURSING: MODELS AND DEVELOPING PRACTICE SETTINGS

4

MODELS OF PARISH NURSING: A CHALLENGE IN DESIGN

Phyllis Ann Solari-Twadell

The church as an integral part of the community has unique qualities that distinguish it as an agency of health or a "health place." One of these qualities is that the mission of any church, irrespective of its denominational orientation, is that of health and salvation. A second is that the intention of the church is to be in relationship with the community, in other words, to respond to the needs of the community effecting change. A third is that the existing internal volunteer structure of the church enhances service opportunities for its members. This structure facilitates the mobilization of volunteers to assist other members of the community in a variety of ways. A fourth identifies the church as the only agency in the community that consistently interacts with an individual from birth to death, serving all socioeconomic groups. A fifth is pertinent to the culture as a mobile society. As individuals move from state to state or country to country for numerous reasons, one thing universally that transfers with the person is their faith orientation. A person new to a community will often locate their home close to a church compatible with their beliefs using the resources at the church for referral to a doctor, dentist or hospital. In the rural community, the church is often the only agency available (Lasater et al, 1986, pp. 125-131, and Schaller, 1985).

Understanding the church as a health place is related to identifying the role a nurse can play as part of the ministry of a church (Westberg, 1988, pp 26-29). An individual whose ministry has a wholistic focus on wellness, disease prevention and health promotion is often called a "Minister of Health." It is important to acknowledge that a minister of health does not have to be a nurse. Volunteers or others who have knowledge, talents and skills in health promotion can be ministers of health. A minister of health who is a parish nurse, however, is a registered professional nurse. The skills, knowledge and experience gained through many years of nursing practice in multiple treatment settings as a paid professional enhances the manner in which the parish nurse is able to practice in the congregation. These properties are best described in the 12 beatitudes of parish nursing developed by Mary Ann McDermott, R.N., M.S.N., Ed.D. (see Appendix A.).

One of the strengths of parish nurse programs is the flexibility of the role and its application in meeting the needs of the community it serves. In one congregation, the parish nurse program may heavily emphasize the educator dimension of the role, while in another congregation, the role may be focused primarily on health counseling or the selection and training of volunteers. In another setting, the parish nurse may serve more than one church. These churches may be close geographically, facilitating this type of operation. These congregations may be of the same or different denominational orientation. Additionally, a parish nurse may serve a church of her own denomination or a church of a different denomination. For example, a nurse may serve a congregation which is Lutheran and her own denominational orientation may be Catholic. This flexibility has encouraged many different ways in which a program may develop. As time passes, experience and knowledge documented and shared will encourage more and more unique ways in which this role can be molded to fit the needs of particular congregations and communities.

Until recently, the best preparation for the role of parish nurse was provided through years of nursing service in a multiplicity of settings (McDermott and Mullins, 1989, p. 29). It has only been in the last year that information and experience on this role has been available through specified nursing orientation and continuing education programs as well as a few undergraduate and graduate nursing programs.

Models

As parish nurse programs are initiated, more and more different models of programming are emerging (Gragnani, 1989, pp 16-19; Buckheim, 1987, pp 4-7; Holst, 1987). In this chapter, the focus will be on four models. They are the hospital sponsored — salaried, congregational based — salaried, hospital sponsored — volunteer, and congregational based — volunteer model (see Appendix B.).

Congregations interested in health ministries often begin with the development of a Health Cabinet or a Health and Wellness Committee (Solari-Twadell, 1988). This Committee often is the group that the parish nurses will relate to in the structure of the congregation.

The first model is the hospital sponsored salaried model (Holst, 1987). Here the nurse is an employee of the institution. The congregation contracts with the hospital for the services of a specific nurse. This nurse's location of practice is then in the designated church or churches.

The single versus multiple church coverage is dependent on the specification of the nurse's employment with the hospital and the needs of the congregation. For example, a nurse may be hired to work half time and be selected to work with only one congregation. Or, the nurse may be hired by the hospital full time and work half time in two congregations, or full time in one congregation.

In order to effectively administer the parish nurse program, the hospital may choose to develop an internal administrative structure. One component of that structure may be the Steering Committee. The purpose of this steering committee is to function in an advisory capacity. The membership on this committee varies. Usually, significant managers who will be instrumental to the development of the program are appointed to serve. This committee may include managers from personnel, public relations, legal, nursing, pastoral care, and finance, along with a member of the medical staff. In addition, a pastor from a congregation in the community may be asked to participate. Initially, the work of this group is more internal as contracts are developed, position description developed and personnel interviews considered. After the first year, the group may meet only once or twice a year to review and advise on the progress of the program. There may also be a decision to disband this committee once the parish nurse program is operational.

A second component of an administrative structure may be a group called the "faculty." The faculty functions with day to day administrative accountability for the parish nurse program. The membership is small, with participation from nursing, medicine and pastoral care. This team is involved in interviewing, hiring, supervising, evaluating and providing continuing education for the parish nurses. Representatives from the faculty interface regularly with the pastors and members of the church who have contracted for parish nursing services. The faculty meets regularly with the parish nurses as a group at the hospital and individually in the parish with the pastor.

The second model is the congregation-based salaried model. Here, a church hires a nurse to work as part of the staff of the congregation. The nurse usually reports to the pastor. This role can be for any amount of hours, though most are half-time positions.

The third model is the hospital-sponsored volunteer. In this model, nurses from particular congregations have been identified as volunteers within their churches. These churches and nurses relate to a particular hospital in the community to provide specific resourcing to the parish nurses. In those instances where a church functioning with a volunteer nurse has a contract with a hospital, the term unpaid may be preferrable to volunteer (Shipman, 1990).

The fourth model is the congregationally based-volunteer model. In this model, a nurse or a cadre of nurses within a specific congregation have been identified to provide certain services to the congregation. Each nurse volunteers according to her availability, anywhere from 2 to 10 hours a week. The focus of the parish nurse role is dependent on the skills and availability of the volunteers.

These models may also be fostered through schools of nursing both hospital and university based, as well as a variety of health care institutions and agencies. As the role continues to be refined, these models will begin to take shape and mature.

In reviewing these models, the following are to be considered: liability insurance, benefits, orientation, supervision — both pastoral and nursing, continuing education, physician availability, peer support, identification of community resources, networking and reimbursement. Each of these items needs to be reviewed in the consideration of the program model to be developed. As decisions are made as to how each of these areas will be addressed, the shape of the model will be defined.

Orientation

Providing of what is known about the parish nurse role, the integration of that into the congregation and the tools to facilitate that process are helpful for every new parish nurse. The hospital-sponsored programs, both salaried and volunteer, are in the best position to provide opportunities in preparation for entry into the role.

Presently, there are opportunities for nurses to be prepared for the role from a number of organizations. The National Parish Nurse Resource Center sponsors a two and one-half day orientation for nurses new in the role. Regionally, colleges and hospitals are beginning to develop orientation programs that vary in length, work and content.

Supervision

Working in a parish nurse role offers excellent opportunity for growth in all areas of one's life. Professional and personal growth are guided when supervision is available in the area of nursing skills and content, and in pastoral counseling skills and content. The agency model, whether that is through employment or volunteering, facilitates the optimum allowance for supervision of both nursing and pastoral skills. The congregation-based model in most instances can provide some pastoral supervision, but lacks opportunity for nursing supervision. Both are important. The nursing supervision will focus more on administrative issues and clinical issues such as documentation, evaluation and particular disease processes. The pastoral supervision will provide opportunity for verbatim and pastoral counseling skill development.

Liability Insurance

The professional nurse who assumes the role of parish nurse will need liability insurance coverage. The parish nurse role has no malpractice history at this point. However, each professional nurse, regardless of the practice location, should be covered by malpractice insurance. The role of the parish nurse is not a "hands on" role, but one focused on education, counseling and referral. Within that role, there is the potential for liability issues to arise. The hospital-sponsored salaried role is the strongest model in addressing this issue. The nurse is covered through the hospital as other nurses employed at the institution. The other three models, the congregation-sponsored salaried, the hospital-sponsored volunteer, and the congregation-sponsored volunteer, require the nurse to carry full liability coverage as an independent through a commercial carrier. However, the cost of this coverage may be assumed by the congregation or hospital as part of the terms of the employment or volunteer arrangement.

It is recommended that as congregations consider parish nurse programs to be part of their ministry, the carrier of the congregation's policy be contacted and informed of the nature of the new parish nurse ministry. This gives an opportunity for carriers to be educated on the role and programs.

The parish nurse is in ministry to serve the members of the congregation and community; however, the skills and talents brought to the role are those of a registered professional nurse. This must be recognized and acknowledged through adequate administrative planning and follow through by the nurse, pastor and congregation. Nurses operating as volunteers must be acknowledged as health care professionals in the act of volunteering.

Continuing Education

The parish nurse role touches on and interfaces with a myriad of disease processes and health issues. The nurse in this role needs a source for continuing education which will help to provide up-to-date information on these issues. The hospital, agency-based parish nurse programs are in the best position to provide these offerings, whether the program is a salaried or a volunteer model. Regular inservice education is enhanced by attendance at one- or two-day outside educational conferences. This expense needs to be included in the parish nurse budget, either within the congregation or the hospital. Other options which can be utilized for continuing education are those available through self-study modules. These are often available through professional nursing journals.

Physician Availability

Parish nurses who are seeing congregation and community members for health counseling will need a physician resource for consultation and at times for emergency referral. It is helpful if this physician is one with whom the nurse has an ongoing professional relationship — one in which the nurse can feel comfortable calling the doctor at any time for consultation. This kind of relationship is most often provided effectively through the hospital model where the nurse is salaried. The physician designated is a member of the faculty of the hospital parish nurse program and fosters that kind of relationship with the parish nurses.

Benefits

Vacation time, sick time, health care, dental and life insurance may be some of the benefits offered today as part of an employment package. As an employer, the hospital or agency is in the best position to offer a comprehensive employee benefit package. The subject of benefits is not an issue for either the hospital volunteer or congregational volunteer parish nurse. Benefits offered through a congregational salaried-sponsored parish nurse program will vary according to the size, resources, financial status of the congregation, and time commitment of the role. The importance is to identify those benefits that will be available through this position early in the development of the role before recruitment of the parish nurse is begun. Negotiation of salary is not completed in isolation of benefits.

Peer Support

The journey of the parish nurses in developing the role is often a solitary one. Peer support is the vehicle which enhances and nurtures the individual nurse on this journey. Vulnerabilities and disappointments can be acknowledged and shared as well as happiness and accomplishments. Through peer support, each not only learns from the other, but identifies and accepts human limitation as part of the individual, not shortcomings for which to be despondent or discouraged. The support provided by other parish nurses is like that of travelers on a similar journey. Recommendations can be made on how to avoid certain pitfalls, and others can suggest positive ways to make time spent on certain projects most efficient. It is the understanding without having to explain the groundwork that makes a peer support group so important to the maturation of the parish nurse.

Identification of Resources

A significant amount of time is spent by most parish nurses in making assessments and providing referrals. It is important that the parish nurse, early in establishing her role, become familiar with all community resources. The identification of these resources can be facilitated by sharing information or by information being given by the hospital. A nurse who is part of a hospital-sponsored program, whether salaried or volunteer, will usually find the development of a resource file to be simplified through the sharing of that knowledge with others. A nurse based out of a congregation having no formal relationship with an agency or institution may have more work initially in identifying referral resources, especially if no one has preceded her in this role.

Networking

For the purposes of this work, "networking" is defined as the reaching out beyond one's regional area to determine what others are doing in a similar position. Networking is making the effort to get to know other parish nurses in other regions or parts of the country. This kind of effort provides an exchange of information which continues the sharing of what is developed, what is working, and how it is being done. It enriches the development of the nurse and the program. This networking can be accomplished through use of The Parish Nurse News or other denominational or association newsletters and through attending the Annual Westberg Symposium on the Parish Nurse or other regional parish nurse conferences.

Reimbursement

During the course of the work of the parish nurse, miscellaneous expenses may occur, such as travel expense for visiting parishioners, the homebound and hospitalized, or purchasing minor equipment or educational supplies. It is important that a determination be made as the parish nurse program is being designed if, in the budget, there will be allowance for the reimbursement of such expenses and if so, how much over what period of time. This kind of information is important for the parish nurse to know in considering to accept the position. Once this commitment has been made, reimbursement needs to continue as an item in the budget.

Designing a Parish Nurse Program
A Journey in Creativity

This section focuses on the importance of intentional design of a parish nurse program. The metaphor of planning a trip or journey has a unique application to this process.

Each parish nurse is on a journey. The journey includes selecting a route to provide for a particular congregation and community a parish nurse program which will respond to their needs. Much as we select different ways to travel to different destinations, we also need to tailor or design our journeys by selecting appropriate methods for each unique trip. "Design" can be defined as the process of creative problem-solving. A design process can be appreciated as a round trip that includes intentions, decisions, solutions, action and evaluation (Koberg and Bognoli, 1981).

In preparing for any trip, the basic requirements must be given priority. Finances, for example, are important. All items need to be thoroughly itemized so as not to be caught with an insufficient amount of money on the trip.

It is important to acknowledge that even though a trip is considered to be enjoyment, there are some unknowns. These unknowns may cause some feelings of fear, especially if you are being creative on your trip. For the fundamental nature of creativity has as its counterpart, fear.

It is also important to remember as one sets out on a journey, travel is a lot more fun when you are not on the run. So take your time.

Problems may arise on the journey. It is important that as a problematic state appears, it is acknowledged as such. Once the problematic state is acknowledged, it is important to identify the essential components of the problem. Once the pieces of the problems have been identified, it becomes easier to identify the skills and methods needed to transfer the problematic state to one that may be more functional.

Creativity is an important ingredient in the design process. Creativity is the art and science of thinking and behaving with both subjectivity and objectivity. It involves being whole — knowing and acknowledging feelings. It requires alternating back and forth between what we know and what we sense and what we can know. There is then an alternating back and forth between thinking and feeling. This leads ultimately to a deeper understanding. One of the hallmarks of creative behavior is curiosity. Curiosity leads to discovery and begets knowledge. From the knowledge comes inventiveness. Inventiveness then encourages variations. Variety then implies a decision. Once decisiveness is applied, action takes place. This leads to consequences and evaluation.

The ingredients of creative behavior begin with self discipline or a freedom from false pride. False pride stands in the way of creativity by inhibiting the designer from asking key questions. It sets up a potential for being untrue to oneself. Self-discipline is the fearless acceptance of who we are. It insures our own development. Self-discipline limits un real, untrue or devious behavior.

A second key to creativity is to believe in one's own ability to succeed. It is important as a designer of a parish nurse program to be able to motivate yourself. Often, if you wait for someone else to move you, it is possible to find yourself headed in an uncomfortable or undesirable direction. It is very important in this work that a parish nurse does not deny her own abilities. The more one believes in her creative potential, the more creative she will be able to be.

Constructive discontent is another key to creativity. A creative problem-solver has a constant developing constructive discontent. At times, it is important not to feel satisfied with a situation. Constructive discontent provides for a seeking of a better way.

A fourth ingredient for creativity is wholeness. All can be more creative if emotions are not stifled, but instead feelings and spiritual insight allowed to enter into the conscious world of our responses.

As a designer of parish nurse programming, the ability to control a habit is another prerequisite for creativity. It is important to know your habits. What habits hinder your creative ability or creative problem-solving?

In reviewing the design process in more detail, the steps are: accept the situation, analyze, define, ideate, select, implement and evaluate. Each of these steps is important in encouraging the development of the program.

Accept the Situation

Acceptance is a word that can be said easily, but is difficult to do. As humans, one of our greatest defenses is denial. Denial can interfere in the ability to see things clearly, identify problems, particularly in ourselves, and realize the full scope of the situation. Understanding the full scope of the situation can be facilitated by active listening. How do others describe the picture? It is important to try and determine the common threads that are reiterated when others describe it. Acceptance requires humility or the ability to "be teachable." It requires the understanding that although I am knowledgeable, I may not have an accurate picture of what the full scope of the situation is at this time. Others may, and I will be well served if I can carefully ask, listen keenly and accept what is unfolding before me, no matter how disappointing or painful it may be.

Analyze

Nurses tend to be action-oriented. There may be a tendency to want to move ahead before all options are considered. It is important to brainstorm, investigate and explore the "ins" and "outs" of a problem. This may be accomplished best by having a few close peers who can be called upon to listen and help reflect on the situation at hand. A peer not so closely tied into a happening may be able to throw a light on the problems at hand that alone one would not uncover. Only when one discovers the "world" of the problem will the full extent of it be acknowledged and all options for resolve be identified.

Define

Defining the problem demands that the essential ingredients of the problem be identified. All significant people associated with the problem need to be acknowledged along with their perspectives. It is helpful to know if this is a recurring problem or an anticipated one-time problem. Again, active listening and peer support as well as supervisory consultation may be important in clarifying the extent, depth, length, significance and consequences of this situation. Defining sets the parameters of the problem and is the beginning of the solution.

Ideate

Once the situation is defined, the scope is determined. Creativity can now be called forth to begin to respond with possible options for achieving the essential goal. All options need to be identified, even those that are not particularly positive. This type of exploring will help in identifying those options that may be best. Again, the assistance of a peer or others of the pastoral staff may be helpful in identifying all possible options. This seeking of assistance may also begin to role-model a healthy way of working together.

Select

After all the options have been identified, the best alternative must be determined. This again is a process that may be accomplished by including others. The ultimate decision may need to be the parish nurse's. Trust of the process in arriving at the top three options may be best accomplished through team discussion. Often, the process is just as important as the outcome.

Implement

Once the best alternative has been selected, it is time to take action and implement. Again, planning for implementation may be important. The factors involved in the implementation should have been identified in the ideating and considered as part of the selection. Also, if the preceding steps have been done with the participation of others on the pastoral staff, their familiarity with the situation may be helpful with implementation of the solution.

Evaluate

Evaluation is a very important part of the design process. It allows for the effects of the plan to be measured. Consideration of this aspect of designing is best to be kept in mind in all the early steps of defining, ideating, selecting and implementing. Evaluation is integral, not an appendage that is tacked on at the end. It is the one way the designer will know how to more effectively proceed on the next leg of the journey.

The design of the journey is not done in isolation. Many people can participate. Our closest partner in that journey is God. The following piece is a favorite and I believe describes how interesting a partner God can be.

Road To Life

At first, I saw God as my observer, my judge keeping track of the things I did wrong, so as to know whether I merited heaven or hell when I die. He was out there, sort of like a president; I recognized His picture when I saw it, but I really didn't know Him.

But later on when I met Christ, it seemed as though life was rather like a bike ride, but it was a tandem bike, and I noticed that Christ was in the back helping me pedal.

I don't know just when it was that He suggested we change places, but life has not been the same since.

When I had control, I knew the way. It was rather boring, but predictable . . . it was the shortest distance between two points. But when He took the lead, He knew delightful long cuts, up mountains, and through rocky places at breakneck speeds. It was all I could do to hang on! Even though it looked like madness, He said, ''Pedal!''

I worried and was anxious and asked, ''Where are you taking me?'' He laughed and didn't answer, and I started to learn to trust.

I forgot my boring life and entered into the adventure, and when I'd say, ''I'm scared,'' He'd lean back and touch my hand.

He took me to people with gifts that I needed, gifts of healing, acceptance and joy. They gave me their gifts to take on my journey, my Lord's and mine.

And we were off again. He said, "Give the gifts away; they're extra baggage, too much weight." So I did, to the people we met, and I found that in giving I received, and still our burden was light.

I did not trust Him, at first, in control of my life. I thought He'd wreck it; but He knows bike secrets, knows how to make it bend to take sharp corners, jumps to clear high rocks, fly to shorten scary passages. And I am learning to shut up and pedal in the strangest places, and I'm beginning to enjoy the view and the cool breeze on my face with my delightful, constant companion, Christ.

And when I'm sure I just can't do anymore, He just smiles and says, "PEDAL."

Author Unknown

So keep pedaling as you design your journey into parish nursing. One thing is guaranteed, it will not be a dull or boring trip.

Summary

The role of the parish nurse is refined as the variety of models and application of the program are developing. The pioneering aspect of nursing is highlighted as professional nurses are creatively addressing all aspects of the current health care crisis as it impacts on the community and particularly those associated with congregations. The nurses, pastors and church members who are taking the risk and incorporating this role in their congregations are most responsively ministering to the needs of their communities. The process of designing a parish nurse program is an ongoing intentional work of the nurse, the congregation and any institutional partners involved. It is an exciting opportunity and the journey will not be uneventful.

Reference List

Buckheim, J. (1987, November). The Gospel according to Roz. The Lutheran Standard.

Gragnani, J.A. (1989, Winter). Parish nurse ministry. Health and Development.

Holst, L.E. (1987). The Parish Nurse. Chronicle of Pastoral Care, 7(1), Park Ridge, IL: Lutheran General Hospital.

Koberg, D. & Bognoli, J. (1981). The All New Universal Traveler - A Soft System Guide to Creativity, Problem-Solving and the Process of Reaching Goals. Los Altos, CA: William Kaufmann, Inc.

Lasater, T.H., Wells, B.L., Carleton, R.A. & Elders, J.P. The role of churches in disease prevention research studies. (1986, March-April). Public Health Reports, 101(2).

McDermott, M.A. (speaker) (1988). Twelve beatitudes for parish nurses [videotape]. Park Ridge, IL: The Parish Nurse Resource Center.

McDermott, M.A. & Mullins, E.E. (1989, Winter). Profile of a young movement. Journal of Christian Nursing.

Schaller, L.E. (1985, January). Why not a minister of health? Church Management - The clergy journal.

Shipman, K. (1990, April 2). Nurse program gives alternative. Farm Week.

Solari-Twadell, A. (1988, Fall). Health and the congregation: A time of renewal. The Chicago Theological Seminary Register.

Westberg, G.E. (1988, November-December). Parishes, nurses and health care. Lutheran Partners.

Appendix A

Models

	Hospital, Sponsored Salaried	Congregation, Sponsored Salaried	Hospital, Sponsored Volunteer	Congregation, Sponsored Volunteer
1. Orientation	X		X	
2. Supervision	X	X	X	
— Pastoral	X	X	X	X
— Nursing	X		X	
3. Liability Insurance	X	?		
4. Continuing Education	X		X	
5. Physician Availability	X	?	X	?
6. Benefits	X	?		
7. Peer Support	X		X	
8. Indentification of Resources	X		X	
9. Networking	X		X	
10. Reimbursement	X			

Appendix B

Twelve Beatitudes for Parish Nurses

Nurses are "blessed" with a variety of gifts that make them uniquely attractive to church congregations striving toward holistic health. However, these blessings, not unlike other talents have their "dark or shadow" side. The following beatitudes should be understood acknowledging that caveat:

1. Blessed be the parish nurse for she is caring!
2. Blessed be the parish nurse for she is available and accessible to most congregations!
3. Blessed be the parish nurse for she is knowledgeable about community resources and the process of referral!
4. Blessed be the parish nurse for she is cost effective!
5. Blessed be the parish nurse for she has a high tolerance for ambiguity!
6. Blessed be the parish nurse for she has had a generalist education and previous employment that have resulted in a broad variety of skills!
7. Blessed be the parish nurse for she is process oriented!
8. Blessed be the parish nurse for she is possessed with a generosity of spirit, both of time and talent!
9. Blessed be the parish nurse for she focuses on priorities!
10. Blessed be the parish nurse for she is committed, dependable and persevering!
11. Blessed be the parish nurse for she has a heritage and tradition of pioneering!
12. Blessed be the parish nurse for she is a believer . . . in God, clients, nursing, herself and in a better world; here and in the hereafter!

(McDermott, 1988)

5

THE DEVELOPING PRACTICE OF THE PARISH NURSE: AN INNER-CITY EXPERIENCE

Jo Ann Gragnani Boss
Jennifer Corbett

*T*wo significant questions emerged from our day-to-day realities after three years of inner-city parish nursing. They were: "Are we making a difference in the lives of people?" and "Are we being made different by the people who have welcomed us into their lives?" The responses evoked by these questions were both simple and complex, clear yet clouded by mystery.

In this chapter, we will review the beginnings of the program, some of the daily realities the inner-city parish nurses meet and attempt to unravel, and as best we can, the forever-unfolding mystery of life we experience. We will describe how the role of the parish nurse has developed and has been interpreted within a contexual relationship in two inner-city hospitals and six parishes.

Inner-City Realities

In July of 1986, after six months of planning and in consultation with Lutheran General Hospital in Park Ridge, the Columbus-Cabrini Medical Center began the first parish nurse program within the city limits of Chicago. "Go where you do the most good." (Corbett, 1988) This was the instruction for mission given by Saint Frances Xavier Cabrini (Mother Cabrini), the foundress of the Missionary Sisters of the Sacred Heart of Jesus who sponsor the Medical Center today. Mother Cabrini responded with insight and courage against high odds to the health and education needs of the immigrants and poor in the early part of the 20th century. It is once again in this arena at the end of the 20th century, that the urban parish nurse has been born, called by name, and now responds by challenging beliefs and cultures. The Parish Nurse Program is seen as a new expression of Mother Cabrini's understanding of health care.

This plunge into six neighborhoods of Chicago was designed to move closer to the marginal and disenfranchised underclass and to offer preventive health services. Parishes selected served those who live on the street, those who do not speak English, those who may be refugees of war, poverty or political dissent, or those who are second-and-third generation victims of discontinued educational and social programs. Acute and chronic problems such as alcoholism, drug abuse, domestic violence, mental illness, unemployment, impoverished housing conditions, hunger and high infant mortality plague many of these parish/community members.

Another factor in choosing a parish was its social and religious commitment to its neighbors and parish members. It is important that the parish church be seen as an advocate, providing opportunities for assisting those who came to its door. It was essential for parishes to be located in multicultural neighborhoods so that the population served reflect the rich diversity of the groups that live in the city. An ecumenical approach has been part of this vision from the beginning. Presently, one of the parishes is Lutheran-Missouri Synod, the remainder are Roman Catholic.

After a series of dialogues with the parish's representative and the Director of the Parish Nurse Program, a formal two-year agreement of commitment was signed by the Medical Center's Vice-President of Mission Effectiveness and the pastors of each program. The dialogues continued as potential parish nurse candidates were interviewed. A mutual agreement of all persons involved contributed to the final hiring decisions.

The attitudes and expectations held by the nurse, the pastor, the parish staff and the congregation about the parish nurse role is important. In all the parishes, even though the nurse may be part time, she is a member of the parish staff and attends their regularly scheduled meetings. In two of the congregations, the parish nurse coordinates the Ministers of Care Programs. Regardless of the nurses' religious affiliation, all the parishes have welcomed them to participate in the sacramental life of the faith community.

While we most often encounter positive overt attitudes and expectations, occasionally we 'bump up' against hidden agendas, negative stereotype thinking and unanticipated challenges. Equality and mutuality as values are still evolving in our churches and society. Effective leadership to empower its people and build responsive communities and responsible members is limited. Religious and social institutions are plagued with attitudes of passivity and dependency, thereby inhibiting people from shaping and directing their lives and imposing dehumanizing roles of servitude — being cared for, protected and defended beyond their real need (Kane, 1989, p. 3). Raising people's consciousness about these rigid and stifling mindsets is not an easy task for the parish nurse. It is met with resistance and painful projections. All of the parish nurses have struggled with these issues of passivity and dependence at different levels within the parish setting.

At the time of this writing, as a result of major consolidation efforts within the Archdiocese of Chicago, one of the parishes will be merging with another to form a new parish. The newly formed parish has invited the parish nurse to join its staff. The process of acceptance will not be automatic. It will require discernment for the needed supportive structures. At yet another parish, one of the nurses resigned after only six months of service. Some of the underlying reasons were: uncertainity of the fate of the parish, frequent changing of pastoral leadership within the parish and choice of the parish nurse to go where she perceived she could do the most good.

Roles of the Parish Nurse

The four functional or service areas of the parish nurse role, i.e., counseling, teaching, advocacy and volunteer coordinator, were described by the inner-city parish nurses as follows:

Counseling

Counseling is a major component of the parish nurse ministry. For the most part, the important skill is listening. Active listening becomes more important with the marginalized people of our society: the elderly, the street person, the poor, the undocumented. Availability and flexibility are of utmost importance — being present at the right time. And who decides the right time? Our schedules or the client? The street person who just happens to call, the mother with a pregnant teenage daughter? We learn flexibility to enable us to put aside our own agendas and to listen and pick out what the client's needs are and underlying what is said, what is the real pain. Counseling is one-to-one: personal, naming names, naming pain, feeling lonely, but being touched and nourished.

The parish nurse does not perform any physically invasive procedures. The Columbus-Cabrini Medical Center covers the nurses' professional liability through their policy. Some parishes have riders on their liability insurance which covers problems related to pastoral care counseling.

Teaching

Within the parish community, teaching — the stamping out of DIS-EASE — takes a long time. Unlearning unhealthy habits and relearning healthier ones doesn't happen overnight. Many physical complaints are voiced and can be associated with loneliness and isolation. Often, people don't want to change. Progress is so slow that at times it goes unrecognized. Being part of a committed parish team helps quiet the voice of discouragement. Together we remember our common call: to be a healing presence to people in need. Life has been hard, and sometimes even unfair, for many that we meet. The hardships wear on them physically and mentally, emotionally and spiritually. They grow old before their time. Classes presented by the parish nurse may be the only entrances into the lives of the people in the parish/community.

Advocacy

The parish nurse is an advocate for the children and adults of the parish community. Working with many of the children and young persons of the parish can mean facilitating support groups for children from homes of single-parent families, teaching health classes to 6th, 7th, and 8th graders, and providing Alatot and Alateen groups. Two other areas in which the parish nurse works as an advocate are food distribution and housing. In working with some tenants who had an unresponsive landlord, one quickly learns how unfair and unhealthy housing conditions can be. Families have been in certain conditions for so long that they come to see them as normal or, out of fear of personal repercussions, have learned to accept inhumane conditions. One tenant had bugs and mice, but stated she had no problems with the landlord. The tenant's child was diagnosed with lead poisoning. A parish nurse needs to offer viable options to people, but she also needs to be honest about what some of the consequences might be for standing up for one's rights: the apartment might get repaired; the family may be evicted; or the rent raised. Advocacy requires that families, church people and neighborhoods come together to bring about this positive and just change in our social systems. Are we and church systems committed enough to work for fuller human life for others through structural change? Will we be able to open our houses and hearts to take in the "the other?" Sometimes, the parish nurse is a mediator; the system or individuals in the system are not always wrong nor the parish/community always right. Helping to interpret the other's point of view is a tedious, time-consuming part of advocacy.

Volunteer Coordinator

The parish nurse program relies on dedicated and caring individuals who are committed to service. The leadership of the parish nurse motivates and helps the volunteers reflect on their experience of service to those who live within the parish boundaries but have no voice. Volunteers provide an essential and often the only link between the outside world and the homebound. They visit the elderly, minister to the sick, and comfort those who have otherwise been abandoned or forgotten by society and churches. They are providing the only human touch that many of these discarded persons experience. Some are overjoyed to see a human face and to have another appreciate the story of their life. Some are angry, needing to be heard. Volunteering takes a special person who is willing to give time and self. Volunteers are critical in implementing the ministry that has been undertaken. They are the lifeline of the continuing outreach and education of the parish community and of the parish staff. In the volunteer as well as with the parish community member, there is a need to recognize and break the chilling grips of poverty and bias. Significant tender loving care is needed to break these embedded cycles. Sometimes volunteering becomes a work-study program. Some of the most effective volunteers are preschoolers who hand out construction paper pumpkins and hearts to hospitalized rehabilitation patients.

Structure and Funding

The Columbus-Cabrini Hospital Parish Nurse Program's overview, structure and organization, as well as the parish nurse job description, is contained in Granger Westberg's The Parish Nurse: How to Start a Parish Nurse Program in Your Church (Westberg, 1987, pp. 70-74). Since that publication, Cuneo Hospital has been closed, thus the name change.

The administrative structure of the program has changed since its beginning. The steering committee functioned for about one year. This committee served as educational faculty on an as-needed basis during the interim search for a new director of the program. For over four months, one of its members became interim facilitator, convening the regular weekly scheduled meetings of the parish nurses. The current director of the Parish Nurse Program reports directly to the chief executive officer of the institution.

As the parish nurses and the program have become more stabilized in the parish/community, both the regular meetings of the parish nurses and the team meetings have decreased. The nurses and director meet twice a month for shared time together. The team meetings (parish representatives, parish nurses and director) have moved from quarterly meetings to semiannual meetings. Here, visions and goals are evaluated, nurtured, restructured and spirits are rekindled. Accomplishments are celebrated.

Initially, the Medical Center provided full financial support of 20 hours per week for each of the six parish nurses and the director. This included salary, benefits and selected supplies. Presently, the hours allocated each parish nurse varies from 20 to 32 depending on the individual's time, commitments and the needs of the parish. Most of the parishes still cannot afford to fund a nurse full time. However, one parish was able to provide funds to increase the nurses's hours an additional four hours, making her total 24 hours per week. Another nurse is in the last year of a three-year declining grant from the Wheat Ridge Foundation, a Chicago-based Lutheran charitable organization that sponsors innovative projects in health, education and social services on an international basis. This grant allowed the nurse to participate full time in the parish along with the Medical Center's increasing support.

Two areas of concern regarding financial matters surfaced: 1) How committed was the Medical Center to the parish nurse program? and 2) Where would monies come from to continue the program beyond the original two-year pilot project stage? During the second year of the program, the Medical Center experienced some financial pressures. When one of the parish nurse positions was placed on hold due to a personnel cutback policy, it became uncertain as to how committed the Medical Center was to the program. A delegation of parish nurses and pastors approached the chief executive officer for clarification. Reassurance was given for continued financial support.

In order to assure an adequate financial base for the program, the Missionary Sisters of the Sacred Heart of Jesus channeled funds through the Medical Center's foundation. To assist their efforts, the hospital initiated seeking additional monies via grants utilizing the hospital's Office of Development. During the annual charity appeal by the Medical Center, the employees were asked to consider donating to the parish nurse program.

We have discovered that promoting the program internally and externally has rewards. Bake sales, donations of Christmas gifts and updates on what's happening in the employee's newsletter have helped to build resource support. Recognition by the Catholic Hospital Association of the Columbus-Cabrini Parish Nurse Program at their annual meeting added to the stability of the program.

For the first two years of the program, $110,000 per year was allocated by the institution. In 1988, $86,200 was the program's actual operating budget. One of the goals of the program is to extend to each of the parish nurses full time status. By the end of 1990, one of the nurses will be funded full-time in the parish by the Medical Center.

Implementing the Parish Nurse Program

While the parish nurses from our program have identified similar goals for their parishes, the implementation of these are unique to each parish. The demographics for each parish are different (Appendix A). With over 400 parish/community member contacts collectively per month, these nurses are uncovering a multiplicity of health care problems. Contacts include person-to-person visits at the parish, home, hospital, clinic or nursing home and communication via the telephone.

Statistical and narrative data are submitted monthly to the director of the program (Appendix B).

It was important for us, as a group, to look at the yearly compilation of data. After examination of some annual statistics, the following conclusions were drawn:

1. There are so many people who come to our attention that cannot be served by one of the functional roles. They do belong within our scope of practice when we broaden our definition and lessen our expectation. These persons take a great deal of time and emotional energy.

2. There are more starving, poor, exploited persons than most of us would have ever believed.

3. The role of parish nurse is becoming rooted in the parishes where we are, and in each parish it has a different flavor.

4. The "accompanying of another" takes a great deal of time. However, it is very much in keeping with the meaning of a Catholic hospital sponsored by the Missionary Sisters of the Sacred Heart of Jesus.

5. It is hard to get volunteers — and we need them and need to think how to do this better. This is an item which will take more problem solving and creativity.

6. It is important to say "no" at times. Saying no and setting limits is difficult to do.

7. It is important to begin by finding out where the parish/community member is, what change they might see themselves making, if any, rather than listening for our own answers, ideas, suggestions for them — first.

8. We spend more time at parish related, community based meetings than we realized. In addition, as a parish nurse staff, we meet twice a month for two afternoons. We will review this to see how this affects the direct service nature of our work, as well as the necessary networking we need to do.

9. We visit more elderly people than we realized. Our current way of accounting for our work does not adequately reflect the numbers of parents and young adults with whom we may interact. If this were more accurate, it may seem less disproportionate and more accurate. However, it is true, we do spend a lot of time with elderly people; their need is apparent to us.

10. We face many factors that impinge on health. Access to health care or getting into the hospital are only starting points of many health issues. Health is broad and focuses inward and outward — beliefs, feelings, relationships, environment, social, political, religious, educational and economic systems. Better health may mean getting a job, finding a shelter, or more schooling.

Some of the accomplishments of the parish nurse program are:

1. Developed an organized system of accountability.

2. Met together regularly for prayer and reflection of God's presence in our everyday lives.

3. Presented public talks about the program to parishes or interested groups.

4. Wrote and produced a 17-minute video and slide/tape production of our work.

5. Developed ways to admit persons with no means to pay into the Medical Center through the parish nurse program.

6. Discovered a number of human resources who have educated us in clinical areas and are willing to accompany us on home visits. We continue to seek ways to link the hospitals with the parish community.

7. Initiated classes at a senior citizen center on weight reduction, nutrition, stress recognition and management. Became involved in schools with Parent-Teacher Association meetings. Presented or coordinated programs on sexual abuse, alcohol and drug abuse, and AIDS education. Coordinated community health fairs and held screenings for blood pressure, diabetes testing, cholesterol, hearing and lice.

8. Began using a theological reflection process in cooperation with another parish nurse program within the Chicago metropolitan area.

9. Selected as one of the winners of the 1989 Achievement Citation, the highest honor awarded by the Catholic Health Association of the United States (CHA). This was in recognition of the accomplishment of Columbus-Cabrini Parish Nurse Program.

What about the accomplishments and changes within the parish/community members? Do we make a difference in the lives of these people?

In these few years, life has not gotten simpler for most of our parish community members. During our scheduled parish nurse staff meetings, we talk about what we have experienced since our last time together, trying to make some sense out of our small presence in these people's lives. We are confronted on a daily basis with a multicultural environment, and complex family configurations on one hand, and overworked social services agencies, multiple neighborhood organizations, financially precarious clinics and hospitals, and invested parish staffs on the other. This dualism/pluralism creates tension which needs to be processed. We have experienced stress, frustration, anger and outrage when these issues go too long without being named and graced with a forgiving spirit.

We do see growth and healing in some of our community people. We celebrate these moments. However, more often we see our efforts, at best, delay a crisis, or even precipitate one.

Practical Spirituality in Helping the Poor

Thomas Merton wrote, ''Do not depend on the hope of results. When you are doing the sort of work you have to face the fact that your work will be apparently worthless and achieve no result at all, if not results opposite of what you expect. As you get used to this idea, you start more and more to concentrate not on the results but on the value, the rightness, the truth of the work itself. And there, too, a great deal has to be gone through, as gradual struggle less and less for an idea and more and more for specific people. The range tends to narrow down, but it gets more real. In the end, it is the reality of personal relationships that saves everything.'' (Forest, 1980, p. 78)

This sense of spirituality can be seen in the writings of Albert Nolan and the views of Gordon Cosby. Nolan, a South African who was a Dominican priest, worked many years in his country struggling against apartheid. Cosby, the founder of the Church of the Saviour in Washington, D.C., strove to balance his personal journey with his activist journey.

The practical view of Cosby points out that the work of caring for the poor only 'sets the stage.' ''. . . our task is to help open up people for Christ to break into their hearts.'' (Wallis, 1986, p. 18) He continues to make the distinction between us doing works of justice and God doing works of conversion.

Nolan, experiencing his own spiritual development, identified four stages of spiritual growth in helping the poor. These stages are characterized by (1) compassion as a starting point, (2) discovery that poverty requires structural changes, (3) realization that the poor must save themselves, and (4) disillusionment at the poor having faults, committing sins, making mistakes, and sometimes spoiling their own cause.'' (Nolan, 1987, pp. 8-12)

''Moreover,'' Nolan states, ''we are not the only ones going through this process. Some will be ahead of us and we may grapple to understand them. Others will be only beginning on the road to maturity in this matter. We need to appreciate their process, their need to struggle further and grow spiritually. There is no room here for accusations and recriminations. What we all need is encouragement, support and mutual understanding of the way the Spirit is working in us and through us." (Nolan, 1987, p. 12)

In response to our own questions: "Are we being made different by the people who have welcomed us into their lives?", parish nurses speak out.

> **Margarita:** In many ways, one of them is being able to appreciate life's worth, not just merely existing as I had been doing for many years. I'm beginning to see life as if I, actually, am contributing rather than just being a receiver. In coming to work as a parish nurse, without knowing, I have begun to grow spiritually. It has been a wonderful experience. It feels as though I've entered a new world. A new world in which I appreciate God, appreciate the gifts that have been given to me and I am beginning to use them. As for the Church, in working as part of the staff of a parish, I've come to see how politics play a big role in the structural hierarchy and sometimes I don't like what I hear or see.

> **Elizabeth:** I believe that I'm learning that many persons are survivors and have coping mechanisms (be it faith or trust in God, family support, grit or whatever) and that changing things does not necessarily make life better. I believe more that God is present in the struggle and not only in the finished product or accomplishment. The people continue to teach me that God is in their lives . . . that God is faithful and knows my needs, desires and potential. "Si Dios quiere" — "If God wants it" is a frequent response that I hear

people say. I used to think that was a fatalistic or false dependency kind of thinking. Now, I tend to believe it comes from a deep trusting place in their heart/lives. I hear it more as an ''If you will, you can heal me'' as in the Gospel.

Karla: This parish nurse work has made me realize the meaning of giving in a different way. It also has made me see the importance of allowing people to make their own choices — I feel like I also have a new respect for what it means to empower people. We must allow people and support people in choices they make for their lives — so that they can begin to feel that they have some control and realize that they are also responsible for them. I always thought I believed in God and I did, but my belief has deepened. When I say now ''I'm going to turn this over to God,'' or ''I'm going to ask God to help me'' with what the answer to some problem is — I really mean it. That's what I do and I wait now for answers. I'm developing more patience.

In summary, we have presented our lived experience of how the Parish Nurse Program sponsored by Columbus-Cabrini Medical Center is developing. This program brings to the poor, immigrant and marginal neighborhoods of Chicago the missionary spirit of St. Francis X. Cabrini.

The cooperative efforts between hospital and parishes have begun to shape a new model of ministry for our times — the parish nurse ministry: teacher, counselor, advocate, volunteer coordinator. This partnership has not been without, nor will it be without, struggles on all fronts and within all of us involved. These challenges — the complexity of the parish/community, the neediness and oppressions of its people, funding and resource maldistribution, time limitations and many others yet unnamed — we admit overwhelm our human spirit. In spite of the odds, we have been able to implement and sustain with "success" six parish-based parish nurse ministries.

What sustains us is the experience, support, courage and hope of each other and of those who have been or are engaged in the struggles with poverty and systems of poverty. Yes, we have been made different and are being made different. Through living our present moments fully, we begin to know that it is God and God alive in history who makes the difference. What is most important is that we become credible human beings in whom the presence of God who loves becomes more clearly the reason for our lives. In that process of conversion we all become partners in the transformation of the world where all can live in freedom.

The authors would like to acknowledge the contributions to this chapter by the other parish nurses in the Columbus-Cabrini Parish Nurse Program. We are grateful for their supportive presence and gentle persuasions.

Thanks to:

Mary Ann Cavagnaro, O.P., R.N., M.A.
Margarita Galvan, R.N.
Elizabeth Gillis, O.S.F., R.N., M.S.N.
Karla Guido, R.N., B.A.
Grace Waters, M.S.C., R.N., B.S.C., M.A.,
   Midwifery Certification: Australia and Africa

Reference List

Catholic Hospital Association. (1989-1990). Annual Report.

Corbett, J. (1989, June 13). Acceptance Speech. Paper presented at the meeting of Catholic Health Association, Seattle, Washington.

Corbett, J. (Ed.). (1988). The parish nurse in the city: Do we make a difference? and/or are we made different? [Text for slide/tape presentation]. Chicago, IL: Columbus-Cabrini Medical Center.

Forest, J. (1980). Thomas Merton: A pictorial biography. Ramsey, New York: Paulist Press.

Gragnani, J.A. (1989, Winter). Parish nurse ministry: Bridging the gap between healing and health care. Health and Development, pp. 16-19.

Guarino, J. (1988, February). Parish-based nurses: A way to help the urban poor. St. Anthony Messenger.

Kane, T. (1989, October). One woman's voice. Call to action. Newsletter, 3900 N. Lawndale, Chicago, Il 60618.

Lundy, B. M. (1989, Winter). Connecting body and spirit. The Lutheran, pp. 9-12.

Nolan, A. (1987, Winter). Four stages of spiritual growth in helping the poor. Helping and Developing. Reprinting with permission from Praying, P. O. Box 410335, Kansas City, MO 64141.

Shore, L. (1988). Within our reach: Breaking cycles of disadvantage. Garden City, NY: Doubleday, Anchor Books.

Wallis, J. (1986, June). A prayer of a chance: Taking evil seriously. Sojourners.

Wallis, J. (1989, July). The call to community: Depending on God's grace. Sojourners, pp. 36-39.

Westberg, G. (1987). The parish nurse: How to start a parish nurse program in your church. Park Ridge, IL: Parish Nurse Resource Center.

Appendix A

Parish Nurse	Members	Economic Mix	Racial/Ethnic Mix	School	Community Service
Chicago Uptown Ministry (near Lawrence & Sheridan—North Side)	50 member worship community (Lutheran-Missouri Synod)	All below poverty line	1/3 Hispanic 1/3 African-American 1/3 Caucasian	Mothers's Support Group Preschoolers—2 half days/wk	Nursing home visitation program Food pantry serves 10,000/yr Youth & teen groups Older adult groups Social services Drop-in hospitality
Holy Family Parish (near Roosevelt & Damen—Near West side)	100 members Roman Catholic	All below poverty line	1/2% Hispanic 1/2% Caucasian 99% African-American	Holy Family Parish School 200 students (K to 8th)	Food pantry serves 200/wk Social services Clothing store Senior citizen program Scholarship program for high school
St. Vincent De Paul (near North side-near Fullerton & Ashland)	1300 members Roman Catholic	Middle pre-dominates 1,000 college students	Hispanic Caucasian African-American	None	Food pantry serving 250 families a month Handout sandwich program for the homeless
St. John Berchmans (Logan Square-near Fullerton & Western)	1200 members Roman Catholic	Some middle income; some below poverty line	70% Hispanic 30% Diverse: African-American, Polish, Pakistani	275 Grammar 150 Preschool	Food pantry Youth center Summer day camp (6-12 yrs)
Providence of God (East Pilsen area-717 W. 18th Street)	800 members Roman Catholic. Average age of members: 22	Low income; some below poverty line	85% Hispanic 10% American 5% African-American	250 Grammar	Soup kitchen feeds 215/week Social services sees 45 persons who walk in/week
St. Ludmilla Little Village (near Kedzie & 24th Street)	1400 members Roman Catholic	Lower income; some below poverty line; 80% undocumented workers	100% Hispanic	320 Grammar	Food pantry/soup kitchen Clothing Room: 48 families/mo 133 persons/mo 1995 meals/yr

Appendix B

In six parishes for the month of October 1989, the parish nurses provided the following services as listed:

Individual/Family Health Services
by Number of Persons Served

	New	Follow-up
A. Home Visits	15	55
B. Office/Church visits	13	28
C. Hospital, Clinic,		
Nursing Homes	7	24
D. Telephone Contact	12	159
E. Advocacy Role	3	3
Total	50	269

Age Profile

0-9	2
10-20	3
21-40	9
41-65	27
Over 65	107
	148

Ethnic Group Served
(excluding telephone contacts)

Hispanic	36
African American	16
Caucasian	96
Asian	0
	148

Referrals

Received by the Parish Nurse from:

Schools	2
Parish Staff	15
Agencies	2
Neighbors	3

Self referred   4
Other: Elders-in-
Distress Program   1

Made by the Parish Nurse to:
Columbus-Cabrini
   Med.Ctr.   3
Clinics   1
Other Agency   1
Parish Staff   1

Screenings:

Blood Pressures,	63 persons tested,	2 referrals
Blood Glucose	8 persons tested,	0 referrals
Cholesterol	65 persons tested,	4 referrals
Lice	173 persons tested,	7 referrals

Programs Given, Facilitated or Coordinated by the Parish Nurse:

Topic	Length	Audience
Stress Management: Sharing of Concerns	3 hrs.	Seniors at CHA bldg.
Culture and Environment: Health Needs	1 hr.	15 - 6th graders
Adolescence and Preparations for Adulthood	2 Presentations	14 - 8th graders
Meeting with the Eighth Grade Class	1 hr.	21 - 8th graders
"The Parish Nurse Program"	1 session	Catholic Charities National Meeting

Health and Healing Seminars	3 1-hr. sessions	Adult parish Community members
Stop Smoking Info. Class: Film, Q&A session with Doctor	1 hr.	7 Adult Community Members
Talk Day: A Discussion (Co-Facilitated with another staff)	2 hrs. every Thurs.	Preschool Mothers 6-10 present
Preschool program (Staffed by volunteers on Thursday)	2 hrs. every Tuesday	6-12 pre-schoolers
Rainbows Support Group	1 hr. every Thurs.	8th graders
Alateen and Alatot Group	Tuesdays	8-19 youths
Halloween Party: Pumpkins distributed by Pre-schoolers	30 min.	Rehabilitation patients at hospital
Halloween Party: Learning Center Kids (15, 7-12 yrs. old)	2 hrs.	Given for Older Adult Group; 19 adults attended

Staff Development/Inservice: Listed in this section are programs attended by the parish nurses for continuing education credit, "in-house" training or pastoral growth and development.

Topic	Sponsor
AIDS High-Risk Adolescent Prevention Project (2 day conference)	National Institute on Drug Abuse & Dept. of Health, Office of AIDS Prevention
Day of Reflection	Columbus Hospital
All Day Parish Staff Mtg.	Parish

Communication/Networking: These activities accounted for a total of 127 hours.

Committees attended by the parish nurses - Social Concern Committee of the parish, Outreach Committee Meeting, Leadership Committee/Fund appeal in the Parish, Little Village Health Council, Staff meetings, Quarterly Board Meetings & Executive Council Meeting, Ministers of Care Meetings, Parish Nurse Staff Meetings.

Liturgical Life: Those activities attended by the parish nurse as part of her ministry in support of the parish community. Funeral Services, Mid-week Liturgy, Staff prayer meeting.

Transportation/Companionship: A total of 41 hours were spent by the parish nurses going with parish/community members. Transportation could include use of own car, parish vehicle or public transportation.

Places traveled to:

Outpatient Clincs	2 trips
Public Aid Offices	1 trip
Doctor's office	1 trip
Hospitals	5 trips
Banks	2 trips
Shopping/Paying bills	1 trip

Communication Tools:
Parish Bulletin Board - Hispanic Hypertension Study and Physical Examinations:
Screening forms (Physicals) - Set up form for the "New Youth Ministry Program"

New Resources: The parish nurse lists agency, contact person, phone number, service provided. Other types of resources such as books, or articles can be listed.

Number of new agencies used as resource	5
Books	1

Narrative Section: Comments are made regarding the month's activities. Listed are the monthly priorities and long-range projects focused on during this time frame.

Jo Ann (30 hr/wk)

Short Range	Long Range
Beginning of Preschool and Mothers' Group: Establishing rapport and initiate trusting relationships.	Reassess involvement with two cases
Home visits, phone on non-attendance	Assessment of select children in pre-school for development concerns.

Analysis/Comments: Very busy month. Preschool is off to a good start. Excellent volunteer help with preschool expert. A Gift! Still very energy consuming for me; however, this time around I feel supported with extra help. Unfortunately, the volunteer will be leaving the area in January. Hope we get a preschool teacher by then. I'm learning more than I ever wanted to know about preschoolers. Mothers' Group developing well. Attendance for this group is higher than last group. Home visits and contacts helping to reinforce commitment.

Exciting to see older adults and our Learning Center kids, ages 7 to 12 years of age, sponsor a Halloween party for the older adults. I was so surprised when the adults, after the kids had modeled playing "Win, Lose or Draw," participated with lots of laughter and delight!!! Will plan future joint celebrations.

Grace (20 hr/wk)

Monthly Priorities

Short Range	Long Range
Same project as last month	Same projects stated last month
To extend my time within pantry where 300 families will be contacted	To extend my educational program to all the grade levels of the school (1 through 7th)
Senior citizens-screening of B/P. Follow-up with individuals who are neglecting their health needs.	

Analysis/Comments: I was very sad that I did not have the opportunity to attend the funeral of J.'s dad because I think that it is important to be present to her and her family. This past month was a busy time, but I enjoyed my personal contact with the associate pastor who accompanied me to visit the homebound and elderly. I recognize how important it is to spend time with them. A few have been neglecting their health. It was necessary to direct them to follow-up with their appointments. They trusted my decisions and it made me more aware of their simplicity and openness for relationships. The homebound and elderly are teaching me about hospitality. They are most willing to share their life stories with me. So far, all of them have a most profound spirituality, and hopefully, I will be able to learn how to love and serve Jesus as they.

Margarita (28 hr/wk)

Monthly Priorities

Short Range	Long Range
Program planning for school children	Day of Reflection for Ministers of Care
Presentation for Catholic Charities	Planning Health related classes for Ministers of Care
Outing with Seniors	Cholesterol Check to be held

Analysis/Comments: More people taking advantage of service being offered at the parish. This month more new persons are being referred to seek assistance and others are just walking in and asking for help. I found out that many people are not aware of my being here because they can't read. Although my assumption is that they only are coming to church when they are in need, the Ministers of Care have requested that I make presentations on different medical problems/diseases for their own benefit.

Karla (24 hr/wk)

Monthly Priorities

Short Range	Long Range
Meet with teachers at grade school	Thanksgiving/Share dinners
Plan health classes and planning for the year	Health classes-grade school support groups for children
Participate in education fair	Illinois Heat & Energy Assistance Program (IHEAP) to
Lice problem	develop parish as a site

Analysis/Comments: I'm not sure where I'm at. This month I have felt very tired-I keep telling myself that part of it is the adjustment to working full-time and I'm sure that is some of it. I feel like I need to pull back so that I have something left for myself. There are many good things happening: we are going to be a site for the Energy Assistance program which I pushed to have here. I am training three to four people to help me. I feel scared I'm afraid that something will go wrong. Thanksgiving Dinner is being coordinated by someone else who is taking over very well.

Elizabeth (32 hr/wk)

Monthly Priorities

Short Range	Long Range
Do annual evaluation	Being "Christmas, Family" contact for an interested organization
Finish office reorganization and client caseload	Concentrate on active family and individual caseload
Reduce number of outside meetings/activities	Collaborate with grade school and youth group in health education

Analysis/Comments: I feel greatly relieved with fewer hours spent in meetings, and less in transportation. However, the hospital and nursing home visits were increased. The AIDS workshop was excellent and I feel like I have new energy to focus on that again. I have appreciated the meetings with the other parish nurse group, but I do miss our time together also. All in all, this month has seemed like a very long month.

Mary Ann (28 hr/wk)

Monthly Priorities

Short Range	Long Range
Anointing of the sick	Needs assessment
Training for new ministers	Combined meeting of Care

Analysis/Comments:
The direction of my work has been changing, there have been some surprises i.e., new Ministers of Care and new

clients. Our long weekend in Wisconsin was wonderful. I had time to sit and enjoy sunsets and sunrises and geese flying — it was great for both body and soul. I've put in extra hours, but have been able to get some of it back which has been good for me.

6

THE DEVELOPING PRACTICE OF THE PARISH NURSE: A SUBURBAN EXPERIENCE

Susan Monaco

Not too many years ago, I was one who had never heard of the parish nurse concept. I had retired from active nursing to raise a family and came to that crossroad many women face around midlife.

It was at that time that I joined my husband for a 10 day business trip. I realized that even I could do only so much sightseeing and shopping, so I decided I would make it an "open-ended" spiritual retreat. I had no big questions, no crisis in my life, I just wanted to spend time in a special way. I found out on that journey that even when you aren't asking questions, sometimes Our Lord gives you answers, or at least a nudge in the right direction.

On our return, I felt both certainty and vagueness. I was confident I belonged in a nurturing profession which was why I had chosen nursing, but I knew I did not belong in the technical arena of hospital nursing. I hadn't had my uniform on in 15 years and more than my waistline had changed in that time. A chance conversation with a guest speaker at church introduced me to the idea of a Clinical Pastoral Education (CPE) program which was available at a local hospital.

I decided to apply, and soon thereafter started my first semester of CPE seeking to discover my options as a woman interested in ministry and healing. CPE was quite a different approach from my experience in nursing school. Back then you learned a technique, for instance, giving injections, then practiced your skills. But in CPE, it was very different. You practiced first and then learned the why and how. I remember how surprised I was when I told my supervisor that I realized that in CPE you do it "backwards" on purpose! You practice your skills of listening, empathy, pastoral counseling with all your humanness and mistakes, and then you go back to the group to process and learn what you did and why you did it.

While a CPE student, I heard about the parish nurse program when Reverend Westberg came to my parish to speak.

All of a sudden, things came together for me. The CPE training, along with my nursing background seemed to fit with the parish nurse role and I wouldn't have to give up my nursing after all.

While I was in the CPE program, I became aware that my pastor had decided to participate in Lutheran General Hospital's parish nurse program. I decided to apply and was chosen for the position. This was in 1986, the second year into the program. Six churches were part of the original group in 1985 and two more were added the second year, my church being one.

I have now been a parish nurse for the last four years at a large Catholic parish of 2,500 families in an older, stable community with a large, older adult population. The church has a grade school, active organizations and several volunteer lay ministries. The staff consists of the pastor, two associate priests, five deacons, principal of the grade school, director of adult education, director of elementary religious education, music director, and parish nurse.

When I first started as the parish nurse, some parishioners wondered why the church needed a nurse. This can
be somewhat difficult to answer because of what people's expectations of nurses are. They expected to see a cap, a stetho-
scope and uniform. Most expected that a parish nurse would
provide traditional "nursing care" of the bed bath and ban-
dage variety. People go to see doctors and other health care
providers when they are sick. Parish nurses are about pre-
vention/wellness and how we can help others accomplish
that which has been a more difficult concept to describe. As
parish nurses, we help channel and direct efforts to assist
people in being more sensible about self-care and health
management. We encourage such things as proper diet, routine checkups and exercise. We are about stewardship of our
whole lives and helping others to help themselves. This ministry strengthens one's focus on serving God by serving one's
neighbor. In this health ministry we define health broader
than the absence of disease. Health includes the physical,
emotional, intellectual, social and spiritual dimensions of life,
which when working in harmony, lead to a sense of well-
being and satisfaction with life (Tubesing, 1983). For example, after a person experiences a heart attack or is diagnosed
as having diabetes, it is very possible that they will make a
conscious effort to make lifestyle changes and thereby raise
their level of wellness. Therefore, wellness is a journey to the
best possible state of health.

This chapter will describe the Lutheran General Hospital (LGH) program and ways in which the parish nurse role
is implemented in a suburban setting.

In the Lutheran General Hospital model, there are
now 12 nurses working in 17 churches of various denominations (Appendix A). Most of the nurses works one-half time
and are employed in a joint partnership between the church
and institution. Most of the nurses work in one church, several in two, and one works in three churches. We have

utilized the model of the church contributing 25% of the nurse's salary the first year and by the fourth year contributing the full base salary. However, as employees of the hospital, we continue to receive benefits and liability insurance coverage. We all go to LGH twice a month (six hours per day) for ongoing education. This time includes medical inservices, resource information, sharing of issues and concerns, time to discuss administrative issues, and time with our physician. The LGH faculty, which includes chaplains, a nurse and physician, plans and coordinates these programs for us.

Some aspects of the CPE model are used when we meet bimonthly at LGH. During interpersonal relations sessions, we discuss verbatims (written conversations with clients and discussed with peers). Since much of our job is listening, we need to be attentive, not only to what the other person is verbalizing, but what other nonverbal messages they are revealing to us. The other half is being attentive to our own feelings and "hooks." I can't tell you the number of times I prepared a verbatim realizing one type of problem and another whole set of issues and challenges came up in the discussion. I never cease to be amazed by the process and have found it to be an important part of my spiritual growth.

One of the issues that frequently surfaces in our group session is that we continually struggle with the "being," since we often get caught up in the "doing." It is very easy to stay on the "busy bee" level. It is much more difficult to stay with feelings. This process of sharing and addressing concerns with the other parish nurses and faculty is integral to my development, both personally and professionally.

Getting Started

The parish nurse program in each church may vary just as each personality, size, etc. of each church is different. One of the strengths of the program is that it is flexible in that the nurses' role uniquely fits the particular needs of each church. Each parish nurse is unique too, having different strengths and gifts, life experiences and previous professional backgrounds. It is important, therefore, to assess the needs and gifts of one's self as well as the parish in order to best utilize these gifts and not duplicate services.

One of the challenges in getting started in the role is to become known to the parishioners as well as to bring health issues to their awareness. This is particularly difficult in a very large parish. An activity that worked very well for me was to organize a health fair.

The fair also provided an excellent opportunity to conduct a survey to discover the educational interests of those attending the health fair. The results of the survey helped in planning for future programs (Appendix B).

Other ways to become known to the congregation may include: an introduction by your pastor at church services, presenting guest speakers at club groups, taking blood pressures at church, writing short articles for the church bulletin and being accessible. Do not underestimate the importance of the latter.

An important part of getting started is collecting data and determining parish and community resources. Much of the first months should be spent visiting community organizations such as the American Cancer Society, American Heart Association, local hospitals, calling or visiting health care services including hospice and local substance abuse treatment centers.

Initially, the best and the worst parts of parish nursing was that our duties were not clearly defined. It was exciting to have freedom to be creative but also difficult not to have guidelines and structure. As we have gained more experience, our role is becoming more defined.

Parish Nurse Roles

1. <u>Personal Health Counselor</u> — discusses health problems and makes home and hospital visits as needed (Westberg, 1987).

This can be accomplished on an informal, as well as a formal basis. Parishioners may casually stop you when they see you at a church function or call just to chat about a health concern. They would inquire about cutting down on cholesterol in their diets, weight management, questions on arthritis or hypertension. Sometimes, they call after they have seen their physician and want more information on their condition, but don't know where to look. You can either give them the information, find pamphlets using terms that are readily understandable, or find a resource for them to use.

On occasion, a parishioner may call with a particular worry, such as upcoming gallbladder surgery, cholecystectomy. More than likely they have heard all the horror stories from friends who may have had the surgery 10 or 20 years ago and are unaware of the more recent improvements in the technology of the procedure. Perhaps they are concerned about the appearance of the scar, or about previous experiences with operations. Old fears and feelings often surface when anxieties arise with new surgeries or illness. The parish nurse is a caring professional who listens and responds to their concerns.

Sometimes, people call regarding how to ask their doctor something. They may need help developing a list of questions for their physician or the parish nurse may even accompany the person to the physician. Other times, a parishioner may have been using a home remedy, or is slow to act on possible serious symptoms and may be asking for permission to phone their doctor. Often, the parish nurse is a sounding board. A mother of a teen may drop in to talk about a son/daughter who has been acting out and she has questions about how to deal with her child. She also needs someone to listen as she shares her feelings about the situation. Even though we may not have all the answers, we may even share the same concerns in our own family, but we can demonstrate caring and understanding.

On the more structured side of health counselor, blood pressures can be taken once a month after the morning services at church. It is helpful to give each person a card from the American Heart Association to record and keep their blood pressure readings so they can notice their own pattern as well as report the readings to their physicians. We have noticed that it is often the last person in line who wants to talk, sharing worries or concerns with the parish nurse.

Parish nurses frequently visit parishioners in the hospital or make phone calls after discharge. These contacts are very important in establishing relationships as well as assessing the need for further assistance. Communication between the parish nurse and other helping ministries in the parish is vital. For example, many parishes have volunteers, Ministers of Care, Stephen Ministries, Befrienders, etc., who visit and may bring communion to the sick in the hospital as well as to members in nursing homes, the homebound, or others in need.

When our Ministers of Care visit people in the hospital, a card is filled out with information about the patient so that the next person visiting knows if they are unable to receive communion due to circumstances such as confusion, nausea or doctors' orders of "nothing by mouth" (NPO). The address and phone number is noted so that further contact can be made by phone to see if they need any further services from the church. Follow-up is very important to the parishioner and family which maintains the caring connection with the church. The parish nurse also assesses how the parishioner and family are doing and mobilizes resources as needed.

A large segment of my time is spent in home visits. After the assessment phone call, I determine if a visit would be appropriate. It is important to visit a seriously ill person at least weekly or assign a volunteer or a Minister of Care for weekly visits. When visiting a very ill person, we minister to the family as well. For example, if the husband is dying, the wife has many concerns which frequently lead to discussion of faith issues. The parish nurse has the unique ability to answer questions about disease and treatment as well as to walk with people through these difficult times. Spiritual issues frequently surface when people are dealing with some type of crisis.

Because of our nursing background, parish nurses may be called upon to serve as advocates with the physicians and other health care providers. We also interface with the other volunteer services of our parish to arrange for rides to the hospital for radiation treatments, meals, or help with chores. However we help, we try to show them that the church personally cares for them.

A group that frequently needs support and respite is the caregivers of elderly, who may be spouses, parents and relatives. By phoning the family, one can find out about the needs of the family member(s) giving the care. These caregivers need a break from the constant pressures on them. For instance, a parish nurse could schedule visits to an elderly woman at a time which might enable her daughter, the caregiver, to take some time for herself to do errands or just to go out and enjoy herself with friends.

The elderly themselves are frequently a group who feel very isolated and are not aware of services offered by the church and community. One of the other LGH parish nurses found that a number of elderly shut-ins could come to the church for a lunch and program if assistance was provided. This created an opportunity for others in the church to volunteer to provide that assistance. This has become a very positive and supportive ongoing ministry in that church.

Another group of people who can feel isolated or not connected to the parish is new mothers, especially with their first baby. These women often have been working until the baby is born and may not have had the time or the interest to join the various groups at church.

I remember visiting a mother-to-be. She had premature labor and was to be on bed rest for the remaining two months of her pregnancy. I visited her weekly, bringing communion. We would pray, and then I stayed as she talked about her feelings and concerns. She also had questions about breastfeeding as she was the first of her sisters or friends to do so. She was very appreciative that I not only listened to her concerns and feelings, but was able to respond to her medical questions.

There are many ways to be with people who are living through difficult times besides the traditional visit. A brisk walk in the early morning to relieve tension can be combined with conversation, meeting for coffee, or engaging in a sport (tennis) or other activity. It is important to be creative and to think of various settings which might be therapeutic for the other person and the parish nurse.

2. Health Education — seeks to promote understanding of the relationships between lifestyle, attitude, faith and well-being (Westberg, 1987).

As previously mentioned, I found that a health fair can be a good "kick off" for the program and I have organized one each year. The twofold objective of a health fair is to 1) raise the awareness of health and wellness, and 2) have an opportunity for the parishioners to see you in a professional role.

Some may question the reasoning of the screenings at the health fair. After all, most everyone in suburban communities has their own physician. But, do people go to their doctors for that seemingly insignificant mole, or do they wait perhaps unnecessarily until they are ill with other symptoms? People often don't look for diabetes or hypertension when they don't even know the symptoms. Thirteen parishioners out of 50 tested at one of the fairs showed an elevated blood sugar level. The skin cancer specialist at the same fair saw approximately 50 people and referred five to their physicians.

Through this health fair, it was discovered that several older adults had not seen a physician for a number of years — they never felt sick and it didn't occur to them to see a doctor to prevent illness. Some of their doctors had retired or died, and they never got around to finding a replacement. They were also very concerned about the costs of tests and doctor visits so they saw this as a good place to get some answers to their questions.

In the last health fair, there were 25 screenings and exhibits plus an assessment booth with an RN to explain any test results or answer questions regarding referrals (Appendix C). The screenings included SMAC-12 blood chemistry (the only screening for which a nominal fee was charged), dermatologist to check for skin cancer, chiropractor, podiatrist, diabetes testing, calculation of body fat, lung function testing, mini EKG, and exhibits on nutrition, hospice, Medicare questions, American Cancer Society, and other community services.

The most gratifying outcome of my first health fair was three individuals who called to tell me that as a result of the testing, silent, but life-threatening conditions of which they had been unaware were discovered. Following a visit to their physician where the screenings were reviewed, one of the three required immediate open heart surgery, another had a very high blood sugar level, and a third was alerted to a kidney problem.

The health fair provides a good opportunity to survey those attending for their interests in future health education presentations. A survey sheet can be distributed with a list of possible topics. The categories could include lifestyle concerns (weight control, stress, nutrition), family issues, topics for adults, parents of teens, young children and subjects titled "When Illness Strikes." The participants can be asked to check off the ones in which they are most interested. This provides data for planning for the coming year's educational offerings. It is important to use a wholistic approach whenever possible as the church is the place where all three aspects of body, mind and spirit can be addressed. For example, a panel on AIDS can discuss the medical, social and pastoral problems concerning those afflicted with AIDS, and another panel, "MEN'S ONLY NIGHT" may talk about male spirituality, male medical problems and male stress. No matter what the program, all aspects of faith and health can be explored.

Try to coordinate your activities with existing organizations. Many churches have a women's club and senior's group. A doctor from the parish could give a presentation on osteoporosis, followed by a luncheon with dishes high in calcium for the women's group. Presentations for the seniors can include "How to talk to your doctor," "What's in your medicine cabinet?", or a talk on "Cataracts and other eye problems." For the Girl Scouts, you could teach the Red Cross "Home Alone" course, the "Babysitting" course, or "First Aid." Another way to bring health education to your parishioners can be accomplished by writing short articles for the church bulletin. Some parish nurses write on how to treat bee stings, swimmers' ear, heat stroke, and various other topics. It can be helpful to have a theme each month for the newsletters or bulletin boards.

3. Referral Source — acts as a liaison to community resources and services (Westberg, 1987).

   Functioning as a referral person is an integral part of this ministry, providing an ongoing, confidential and professional source of assessment and referral. The parish nurse is not viewed as a primary health care giver, but as one who facilitates and enables people to use appropriate resources.

   Times of crisis are often times of confusion for a family. The parish nurse can be the family's "legs" in identifying the different options. Perhaps grandma is coming out of the hospital and the family is looking at the different types of housing available. Questions such as, what about home health care versus nursing home, what is the cost, levels of skill needed, what services are available and whom do you contact plague family members. Sometimes, they are unsure of the issues or questions to ask.

   You may want to accompany the family to look at a prospective nursing home. Beforehand, discuss what to look for and specific questions to ask the administration. This is a big decision, and often the son/daughter expresses feelings of sadness, guilt and/or loss as they talk after the visit. Many people naturally turn to their church when they need help. Most like personal referrals. The question heard most is, "Maybe you know _____?" The parish nurse can be the constant, confidential and professional advocate for the family.

   Many referrals are made to Alcoholics Anonymous, support groups, home health care, live-in caregivers, treatment centers, and physicians. If you don't have the information at hand, your best response is "Let me get back to you." Other parish nurses, such as I have found at LGH, and church and community networks are a tremendous resource. It is recommended, if possible, to give a couple options for referral. In this way, the individual can make the final choice as to which fits their needs.

It is just as important to be able to network and communicate within the parish organizations and volunteer groups as the community services. When making the follow-up calls of parishioners discharged from the hospital, try to link them up with the appropriate ministry to get the help they need. Perhaps, assign a minister of care to bring communion, a friendly visitor, a driver for treatments at the hospital, or a shopper. One parish has one group of volunteers sponsored by the women's club for short-term needs, whereas the older adult ministry supplements services if the needs are long term.

One Roman Catholic Church has a medical supply closet which is coordinated by the parish nurse. Used home health aids such as walkers, tripod canes, wheelchairs and commodes have been donated. These items are loaned out to anyone who needs them for as long as they need them. The parish nurse can be a vital person who is able to connect people with needs to the most appropriate resources in the church and community.

4. Facilitator — recruits and coordinates volunteers and support groups within the parish (Westberg, 1987).

Volunteers are truly the backbone of a successful and meaningful ministry. "Now there are varieties of gifts, but the same Spirit; and there are varieties of ministries, but the same Lord." 1 Corinthians 12:4. With the varied ministries come many different volunteers with diverse motivations.

One of the many interesting things about people is that they come in different sizes and shapes, different abilities, personalities, and likes and dislikes. As the coordinator or facilitator of the volunteers, we work with and through these groups to accomplish our goals. One priority in achieving these goals is to understand as much as possible why people do things (or do not do them). One way of putting the right volunteer in the appropriate job is to know what motivates them or what gives them energy to do a task.

As parish nurse, one of my roles is to provide training for new volunteer ministers and continuing education for the lay ministers who visit the sick and homebound, coordinate and organize new volunteers and support groups. During my second year, a bereavement committee was started. A fellow parishioner who had been active as a hospice volunteer and myself discussed the goals and methods and planned the training sessions for the volunteers. We established the following goals:

1. To develop teamwork among the pastoral staff, funeral directors, lay ministers and the community.

2. To assist the grieving in planning a liturgically appropriate and meaningful (personal) funeral rite.

3. To assist the bereaved and establish a relationship of ongoing care and support from the parish family.

When the church is notified of a death by the funeral home, the secretary gives a copy of pertinent information to the bereavement ministry coordinator (parish nurse). I then contact the bereavement minister giving the family contact name, phone and address. The volunteer bereavement minister calls the family to ask if they would like to give any special input for prayers at the wake, readings and songs, etc., for the funeral. If so, a time is arranged for the bereavement minister to come to the home. Otherwise, the minister assures the family that the presiding priest will take care of scriptures and the Resurrection choir director will select the music. The berevement minister also may assist the family with other requests. For instance, one family needed someone to stay at her home during the funeral; another needed a wheelchair for the mother who lost her newborn. This is only one part of this ministry. The important focus is the ongoing one-on-one support to the spouse or other family members during the grieving period, which may last for sometime. It is particularly important to follow-up with people on special holidays and anniverseries.

In one parish, an ongoing caregivers support group began as response to several parishioners who wanted to talk with others who had the same concerns. Several people who were taking care of aging parents or spouses, some of whom had Alzheimer's disease, were asked to come to a special presentation and discuss the possibility of a support group. It was not long before a monthly caregivers support group was formed.

Another group is the Parish Support Team for Substance Abuse (Svendsen, 1986). This team provides intervention through awareness, education and providing resources for those addicted as well as their families. It is estimated that one out of ten in any large congregation is afflicted with this disease. The need for support and education is very apparent.

Other parish nurses have initiated support groups for weight loss, stop smoking clinics, young mothers' groups, parenting classes, grief support, and support for health care professionals.

Unexpected Crisis

As mentioned previously, the role of the parish nurse is flexible . . . sometimes more than others. Unusual or unexpected crisis such as a flood or other natural disasters necessitates an unusual response in the form of Christian outreach and aid for many families who need help.

Our town experienced a late summer flood. The rains started on Thursday and Friday. By Saturday, many sewers and streets were flooded over the curbs and into the homes. On Sunday, our pastor asked a sparsely filled church (due to the flood) to respond to the need of our neighbors by signing up to help with cleaning, cooking and serving food. That was the beginning of our lists. We had no idea of the extent of the need nor the magnitude of the giving that was to take place over the next six weeks. Some of the cleanup efforts, rebuilding and exchange of furniture lasted for months.

The pastor asked me to help answer the phones and coordinate the clean up teams with a fellow parishioner. We put up signs at the tetanus inoculation center which simply read: Free clean-up help and lunch at Visitation church. We had an immediate response. The pastor also asked the women's club to provide lunch. They fed over 500 people every day for the next two weeks. Another church a few blocks away cooked dinner so that those who had no electricity or water could have two hot meals every day. Parishioners and many others from the community donated the food. Others donated "start up kits" which consisted of staples such as salt, sugar, flour, cleaning supplies, bleach (for clean up) and canned foods. Others donated clothing for our clothing closet. Still others called the church to give such articles as bed sets, washers, dryers, and freezers to those who had experienced the greatest loss.

My task was to link the people who needed clean-up help or furniture with those who had volunteered to help. Many people called to volunteer their time in whatever way they could be of help. Phone calls were made to the local high school football coach, and another high school's soccer team to ask their help to lift water-soaked furniture and appliances. The Viet Nam Veterans came with their wives to work. There was much to do. Water logged furniture, cartons of Christmas ornaments, boxes of stored memorabilia and rugs had to be dragged out of basements and crawl spaces. Others scrubbed floors and walls with disinfectant.

Our church was also the site where the Red Cross processed the flood victims to receive aid.

After the flood waters had receded, there were still the emotional issues. Can you imagine how you would feel if you lost not only furniture and clothes which could be replaced, but also lost precious treasures such as pictures collected over a lifetime reflecting the special events of your family? In the weeks following the flood, I contacted the Red Cross post trauma counseling service and scheduled four support groups led by professionals to deal with the normal fears, depression and anxieties following such traumatic experiences.

Groups were set up according to streets so the people who experienced the same type of damage would be grouped together. The discussions centered on what were normal reactions to the crisis, feelings, coping methods, what to expect and practical resourcing such as how to apply for federal loans.

We worked with hundreds of volunteers who helped in a variety of ways. I have never seen such outpouring of kindness and cooperation. Part of my work as parish nurse was to match the strengths and gifts of each volunteer with the needs presented. Volunteers need to feel support. All do better if they feel good about what they are doing (Litwin and Stringer, 1968).

Some ways to show appreciation are: provide money for training and retreats, recognition dinners, worship services in honor of volunteers and notes of appreciation in the

Sunday bulletin. It is also important to recognize your volunteers as individuals. This can be done by sending cards to celebrate/acknowledge special occasions, notice when they don't show up and follow-up to find out why, express appreciation for their efforts and acknowledge outstanding achievements. Finally, it is important to offer your support by listening to them and offering opportunities for their personal growth wherever possible.

Then and Now

Looking back over the last few years, much has stayed the same and much has changed. There is still the challenge of balancing the pastoral and medical aspects of the parish nurse's role as well as explaining to those who have never heard of this new concept what exactly a parish nurse does in a church. The needs of the elderly, young families and those who seek help remains constant, but these needs are now being met in new creative methods by this unique staff member.

The approach has shifted from the first few months on the job. As we began, many parish nurses used educational classes to establish our identity. Frequently after the first year, the position develops into the intimacy of one-on-one relationships rather than reaching out primarily through groups. At the start we were anxious about how we were going to fill those 20 hours. That was a short-lived anxiety. We were soon setting limits and boundaries. Time must be carefully scheduled, duties prioritized. As our networking expanded, so did our community interactions. We became an important link with community resources, receiving calls for a volunteer, a wheelchair or hospital bed. At other times, the County Human Services Department has referred their clients to our ongoing church support groups. The requests are as varied as the people in the parish.

Overall, I am a parish nurse because I enjoy it. I'm one of the lucky few who have been blessed with the opportunity to have a job that fulfills so many of my own needs and which gives me the privilege of helping others meet theirs. Being a parish nurse has been a journey toward self-discovery. Every person I have met has enabled me to come that much closer to the fullness of who I am and who God calls me to be. It is through the people of my community that the parish nursing program has been defined. As the Lutheran General Hospital program has matured, so too have I.

Reference List

Litwin, G.H., & Stringer, J. (1968). Motivations and organizational climate. MA: Harper & Row, Harvard Business Press.

Svendsen, R. (1986). Chemical health. Minneapolis, MN: The American Lutheran Church.

Tubesing, D. A. (1983). The Caring Question. Minneapolis, MN: Augsburg Publishing.

Westberg, G. (1987). The Parish Nurse: How to start a parish nurse program in your church. Park Ridge, IL: Parish Nurse Resource Center.

PARISH NURSE PROGRAM SUMMARY
Appendix A

Congregation	Membership	% Under 65	% Over 65	Est. # of Indiv. Clients Per Month	Est. # of Group Clients Per Month	Hours per Week	Year began PN Program
Grace Lutheran	1,917	84%	16%	60	150	20	1985
First United Methodist	750	70%	30%	30-50	50-60	20	1985
Lake View Lutheran	83	68%	32%	20	50	10	1989
Lake View Presbyterian	91	71%	29%	15-20	30	10	1989
Glenview United Meth.	1,099	80%	20%	43	20-30	20	1989
Lutheran Church of Atonement	1,094	94%	6%	80-90	75-80	40	1985
Visitation Catholic	7,500	65%	35%	45	45-50	20	1986
Epiphany United Church of Christ	120	60%	40%	15-20	none	7	1988
Concordia Ev. Lutheran	100	50%	50%	15-20	none	7	1988
Joyce United Methodist	100	50%	50%	15-20	none	7	1988
Our Saviour Lutheran	3,104	93%	7%	30-50	60-80	20	1985
Our Lady of Ransom	8-10,000	70%	30%	40-50	50-60	20	1985
Ebenezer Lutheran	1,144	42%	58%	68	468	10	1988
Immanuel Lutheran	709	50%	50%	59	484	10	1988
Glenview Community	1,800	80%	20%	105	450	20	1986
St. Isaac Jogues	5,500	75%	25%	125	300	20	1987

Appendix B

Participant Evaluation Form

Please check off your response(s):

1. How did you learn about our health fair?
   ___ Flyer ___ Poster
   ___ Word of Mouth ___ Newspaper
   ___ Newsletter ___ Other

2. Which of our health fair booths were the most interesting and useful for you?

___ Heart/Hypertension	___ Mini EKGs
___ Dental Booth	___ Blood Donations
___ Vision/Hearing	___ Lung Function
___ Nutrition	___ Chiropractor
___ American Cancer Society	___ Telecare
___ Safety Booth	___ Hospice
___ Substance Abuse	___ Osteoporosis
___ Vision and Hearing	___ CPR
___ Percent Body Fat	___ Optometrist
___ Senior Services	___ Podiatrist
___ Respite Care	___ Diabetes
___ Pharmacist	___ Blood Testing
___ Skin Cancer Screening	___ Body Mechanics

3. What would you like to see that was not offered?
   _____
   _____
   _____

4. Were the people who assisted you helpful/professional?
   _____
   _____
   _____

Appendix B (continued)

5. How helpful did you find the health fair?

_____

_____

_____

Thank you for taking time to answer these questions for us!

Enjoy your day!

Additional comments: _____

_____

_____

_____

_____

_____

_____

_____

_____

_____

Appendix C

Attendance/Referral Evaluation Form

Evaluation of the number of people who attended each booth and the number of referrals made at each booth.

Tally Sheet

Booths Attended	Number of People	Number of Referrals
1. Registration	_____	_____
2. Vision	_____	_____
3. Hearing	_____	_____
4. Nutrition	_____	_____
5. Percent Body Fat	_____	_____
6. Safety and Substance Abuse	_____	_____
7. Senior Services and Respite Care	_____	_____
8. Telecare	_____	_____
9. Chiropractor	_____	_____
10. Lung Function and Referral	_____	_____
11. Blood Pressure/Heart Rate Screening	_____	_____
12. Mini EKGs	_____	_____
13. Blood Donations	_____	_____
14. Hospice	_____	_____
15. Osteoporosis	_____	_____
16. CPR	_____	_____
17. Cataract and Glaucoma Screening	_____	_____
18. Dentist	_____	_____
19. Podiatrist	_____	_____
20. Diabetes	_____	_____
21. Pharmacist	_____	_____
22. Physician	_____	_____
23. Blood Testing	_____	_____
24. Body Mechanics	_____	_____
25. American Cancer Society	_____	_____
26. Summary	_____	_____

7

THE DEVELOPING PRACTICE OF THE PARISH NURSE: A RURAL EXPERIENCE

Jan Striepe

"*I* may not know exactly where I'm going, but I know I'm not lost!" I have said that phrase many times since 1985.

I entered nursing because I wanted to be in a caring profession. In my basic nursing education at Fairview Hospital School of Nursing, instructors and chaplains taught about the significance of faith in a person's life, especially during illness.

In recent years, scientific research affirms what theologians have said for centuries. Spiritual nurturing contributes to improved life satisfaction and quality of life, improved health, reduced functional disability, and lower levels of depression (Magan and Haught, 1987).

As a parish nurse-minister of health, I have been privileged to be with people during many different events and situations. The church is involved in the process of people's lives at all age levels, periods of development, times of joy, and times of sorrow.

The church is the original health and healing organization. Since the church has historically been associated with health and healing, it is an ideal setting for health promotion and wellness programs to take place (Miller, 1987).

After I had begun a parish nurse service in 1985 at Trinity Lutheran Church (350 members), located in Spencer, Iowa, I was certain that I was not unique. I thought other nurses would become parish nurses if they received support, educational opportunities, and some tangible incentives such as resource books, pamphlets, and an educational stipend. Also, I felt that parish nurses could be valuable health resources in small congregations in rural areas.

In this chapter, I will discuss several aspects of the rural network: the characteristics of Northwest Iowa, the history of the network, characteristics of the nurses and churches, and models of parish nurse services. Also, an overview of the accomplishments of the nurses and some of their satisfactions and frustrations will be reviewed. The last section will discuss special considerations for rural parish nurse services and networks.

Characteristics of Northwest Iowa

Before attempting to initiate a rural parish nurse network, I considered characteristics of our rural area. Farming is the backbone of the economy. Since 1985, the economy of Northwest Iowa has been very depressed due to the farm crisis. The proportion of elderly in the rural population is greater than in urban areas, and it is expected to rise. Also, elderly depend on health services more and have higher rates of chronic disease than other population groups.

Demographically, Iowa ranks in the top five states in the proportion of people 60 years of age and older. Twenty-two percent (22%) of the population of the 14-county area of Northwest Iowa are age 60 and over, and 8% of those are age 75 and over. This area is not culturally diverse, as the majority of residents are white Anglo-Saxon American.

The population of the area is dispersed through numerous small towns and farms. The average population of the counties is 15,000. Most of the counties have one or two towns with a population of 5,000 to 10,000, and eight to ten towns which average 500 people.

The data about hospitals, churches and the economy is also significant. All of the hospitals in a 60-mile radius of Spencer are small (ranging from 20 to 100 beds), with many of them struggling financially. Most of the hospitals' governing bodies are city or county, and therefore, do not have an affiliation with a church denomination. The churches in the area range from very small, with less than 200 members, to very large, with more than 1,500 members. The majority of these churches have a membership of 300 to 400.

Several other factors are relevant. None of the small towns have a physician. Many nurses work part time, and many nurses were already using their nursing skills and knowledge within their church and community. In effect, they were functioning as "informal parish nurses."

The preceding information assisted me in formulating criteria and a plan for establishing a parish nurse network.

History of the Parish Nurse Network

St. Luke's Regional Medical Center (SLRMC) in Sioux City, Iowa, was the catalyst for assisting nurses to initiate parish nurse services. This occurred because of the efforts of Jan Burg, R.N., and the board members of the Wholistic Health Services. In 1984, Jan started a nurse-in-church program after hearing Granger Westberg's presentation.

In 1985, several key events occurred. A workshop, "Parish Nurse: A Needed Concept," featured Granger Westberg, Mark Laaser, Jan Burg, and myself as speakers.

The workshop generated much interest among nurses, pastors and the administration of SLRMC. SLRMC provided $20,000 to the Wholistic Health Services Board to be distributed as parish nurse stipends. The money was distributed evenly to 11 parish nurses: 8 nurses in Sioux City and 3 rural nurses.

More Sioux City nurses began as parish nurses in 1986 when SLRMC provided another $20,000. Since 1987, SLRMC has not provided stipends, but has supported the parish nurses by providing health educational pamphlets and meeting rooms.

In 1986, I began exploring the possibilities of a rural network and the funding for a network. Since a hospital-based parish nurse network was not feasible, I contacted Greg Anliker, Director of the Northwest Aging Association, to discuss my ideas. His enthusiastic response led to the writing and funding of a grant from the Northwest Area Foundation in St. Paul. The one-year project had as its goal to establish a network of ten parish nurse programs in a nine-county area. The parish nurses emphasized health promotion and health maintenance of the elderly.

An overview of the project's stipulations include:

Definition of a parish nurse - a registered nurse (RN) functioning as a wholistic health educator, resource and referral person in a church setting;

RN's would receive:

- $500 stipend for attending educational sessions
- Resource books/pamphlets
- CEU — certified educational sessions (approximately 50 hours)
- Assistance from parish nurse coordinator

RN's would agree to:

- Attend the educational sessions
- Volunteer approximately four hours a week
- Maintain data about clients and activities

Churches would agree to:

- Support and encourage the parish nurse service
- Provide office space, phone and office supplies
- Consider future funding of the parish nurse service through salary and/or expense reimbursement

The project was very successful! A summary of that beginning year includes some interesting statistics. There were 12 parish nurses in the nine-county area. Partial data about their activities include: 2,052 client visits at the church; 379 home visits; 85 health promotion presentations; and 273 referrals to physicians, health or social agencies. In addition, they wrote health articles in the church newsletters, maintained bulletin board displays, and even organized health fairs.

After the project was completed in the fall of 1987, I continued as a volunteer coordinator for the network. We had regular "share meetings" and a mini-newsletter.

In the fall of 1987, after being a volunteer parish nurse for over two years, my church voted to salary me as its parish nurse for 20 hours a week. At the same time, I had been accepted in Iowa Lutheran Hospital's Minister of Health Education/Intern Program. Half of my half-time position was salaried by the program and half by my church. My church had a pastoral vacancy during my internship, and I consistently worked more than 20 hours a week!

During this time, I continued to have nurses and pastors ask me about helping them start parish nurse services. These requests urged me to obtain more funding to develop and expand the network.

In 1989, the W.K. Kellogg Foundation approved the Northwest Aging Association's grant application for a three-year parish nurse project. The intended outcomes of the project include:

1. Provide educational programs, support groups, and ongoing resourcing of 25 established parish nurse services.

2. Initiate 10 new parish nurse services.

3. Provide a wholistic nursing core curriculum.

4. Provide a specialized geriatric curriculum.

5. Provide resources for parish nurses (Appendix A).

6. Assist in the establishment of a Health Ministries Association.

The project is community-based, involving several collaborators. Interacting in the project are two Area Agencies on Aging, community colleges, St. Luke's Regional Medical Center, Northwest Iowa Mental Health Center, and several health, social and educational professionals who serve on the Advisory Task Force. In the rural area, coalitions are essential for parish nurses and for parish nurse networks.

Characteristics of the Nurses

There are 36 parish nurse services in the project; however, there are 41 parish nurses because five of the churches have two nurses sharing the responsibilities.

The following information summarizes facts about the 41 parish nurses:

1. Thirty-three nurses are employed in another area of nursing such as staff nursing in hospitals and long-term care, community health, school nursing, and nursing education.

2. Graduates of diploma or associate degree programs - 31.

3. BSN nurses - 5.

4. Masters-prepared nurses - 5.

5. Serve as parish nurses in the church of which they are a member - 40.

6. Salaried part time by their church - 3.

7. Expense reimbursement budget for supplies - 8.

8. Majority have not actively pursued a salary from their church, but plan to do so in the future.

9. Majority average four hours a week as a parish nurse.

10. Majority have functioned as "informal parish nurses" in the past.

11. Parish nurses who are married to a pastor - 5.

Characteristics of Models of Parish Nurse Services in the Project

There are several models which have been developed by the nurses establishing their parish nurse service. The models are solo parish nurse for a congregation, co-parish nurses, parish health coordinator, "Marcus model," and parish nurse for several congregations.

The majority of parish nurses in our area are solo parish nurses. Although many of them use other professionals and lay persons to assist them with various parish nurse activities and goals, this is done on an intermittent, informal, "as needed" basis. There are several reasons for the prevalence of this model. The main reason is that in small towns with churches of about 200 members, there may not be another nurse in the congregation. Or, the other nurses simply want to assist on an intermittent basis.

Also, many nurses are in congregations of less than 500 members and are able to affect members' lives by working four hours a week. In comparison to the above example, a nurse would need to work 20 hours in a congregation of 2,000 to affect a comparable number of members.

The co-parish nurse model has worked well for several nurses. The nurses work closely as a team to implement their activities. They often take turns with the parish nurse office hours and home visits. In some cases, one nurse coordinates the educational programs, writing articles, and office hours; the other nurse makes home visits or telephone calls to the homebound members and members who are ill. An advantage to this model is that the nurses develop a support system for each other.

Three parish nurses in our area have organized their parish nurse service by establishing themselves as the parish health coordinator. Two of the nurses are members of large congregations, and one is in a smaller congregation which has seven other nurses. As parish health coordinator, they organize other nurses to implement the health activities in their congregation.

The "Marcus Model" is a unique situation. In Marcus, Iowa (pop. 1,200), there are five churches. The pastors of the churches and two nurses spearheaded a plan to have a parish nurse at each church. After sending out letters and holding meetings, this very rural community now has implemented its plan. The nurses met at least monthly in the beginning so that they could coordinate programs and activities. For instance, one nurse had expertise in cardiovascular nursing and offered to present Healthy Heart programs at all the churches. Another nurse was very interested in home safety assessments, especially with the elderly. She taught the other nurses and other volunteers how to do those assessments. It will be interesting to document the activities and determine the impact of the activities on their congregations and community.

Characteristics of the Churches in the Network

There are 36 churches enrolled in this project. The characteristics of the churches are:

1. Denominations represented — 7. These include Baptist, Roman Catholic, Evangelical Lutheran Church in America, Lutheran Church Missouri Synod, Methodist, Presbyterian, and United Church of Christ.

2. Congregations of less than 1,000 members — 25. Of the 25, 18 have less than 500 members.

3. The churches in very rural towns, a population less than 5,000, have 20% to 40% elderly members.

4. Churches with more than 50% elderly members — 5.

5. Majority do not have a separate health cabinet or committee, but work with established church committees.

Accomplishments of the Parish Nurses

Since January of 1990, the 41 parish nurses involved in this project have documented their activities on a standardized form. Preliminary data for six months illustrates that the nurses are functioning well in the various roles of a parish nurse. These recent statistics include over:

1. 2,500 church visits

2. 200 home visits

3. 800 telephone calls

4. 120 presentations

5. 110 referrals to physicians

6. 50 referrals to health agencies

Support groups have been initiated, and hospitalized members and members who are residents in nursing homes have been visited by parish nurses. This data was not available at the time of this writing.

Since Sioux City nurses are in the network, there are 13 parish nurse services from a rural-urban area, 19 parish nurse services in very rural towns with a population of 5,000 and below, and four parish nurse services in rural towns with populations of 5,001 to 15,000.

Comparing the initial data of the very rural and rural nurses with the data of the rural-urban nurses, the parish nurse activities are similar. However, the initial data suggest that very rural/rural parish nurses have more of the following activities than rural-urban nurses: home visits, support groups, exercise classes, and transportation for members.

The data are not surprising since smaller towns do not have YMCA/YWCA or health club facilities for people to attend exercise classes or health institutions providing structured support groups. Also, transportation is a common problem for the elderly in the rural area.

The preceding data about statistics and activities are important. However, the people that the parish nurses assisted tell the real story. Here are a few examples:

An elderly woman was in need of home health assistance, but she refused to allow the community health nurse and nurse aide to assist her since she thought their services were "welfare." The parish nurse visited her at home and was warmly received since the woman knew she was from her church. By the end of the visit, the woman had agreed to assistance from community health professionals and said she would welcome visitors from their church.

Another nurse initiated "We Care" volunteers who would assist church members with needs. Several nurses initiated exercise classes at their churches including exercises for seniors; the fellowship was as important as the exercise!

In one small town of 800 people and with seven churches, the parish nurse began having monthly health presentations. People from all denominations attended those programs! Grief support groups were very helpful since the small towns in Northwest Iowa had not had them before.

There were many instances where the parish nurses responded to a church member's crisis situation by arranging for other members to assist and by contacting health/social agencies. For instance, they have assisted elderly persons' placement in nursing homes. The rapport of the pastor and the nurse with the elderly person eased that difficult decision and transition. This is especially important since, many times, the elderly person did not have children living in the community. Some elderly persons living on a fixed income, who would qualify for programs such as fuel assistance, did not seek help; instead, they stopped buying their medications to pay their utility bills. The parish nurse assisted by educating and supporting that person to complete the forms or referred the person to the elderly advocate of the Aging Association.

There are many examples of parish nurses enhancing the caring community of their church. They have worked in cooperation with the church committees and pastors to assist members in need. Many of the parish nurses initiated or expanded prayer chains in their congregations. Other parish nurses organized lay visitors or attended the Stephens Ministry Training to coordinate and initiate Stephens Ministers in their congregation.

The health program topics which nurses have given or coordinated have been diverse. Many of the nurses implement a congregational interest survey before planning the topics. Also, most of the nurses utilize the meetings of established church groups for their presentations. A few of the parish nurses have coordinated a program or a series of programs offered in the afternoon or evening. Some parish nurses give health presentations at the local senior center.

Some program topics are:
Coping with stress
Healthy eating
Loss and grief
Farm safety and pesticides
Caring for the caregiver
Parenting
Wholistic health
Faith and feelings

Classes on specific illnesses such as heart disease, arthritis, diabetes, premenstrual syndrome, and others

The parish nurse services in this network are diverse. I encourage the parish nurses to develop their service according to their own strengths and congregational needs. In addition, I remind them to establish their own parameters of activities. For example, some parish nurses do many presentations, while others do only a few. Some parish nurses make many home visits while others do not make home visits, but rely on volunteers and/or telephoning. Some parish nurses have many clients come to the church during their office hours. The parish nurses who had only a few appointments decreased their office hours to monthly and concentrated on other needed activities.

Another accomplishment of the parish nurses is completion of the wholistic nursing core curriculum and the specialized gerontology course. The core curriculum is equivalent to college credits. It is offered during a three-day course at a Bible camp. The one college credit gerontology course is offered in the evening for four consecutive weeks.

Satisfaction and Frustrations of the Parish Nurses

The satisfactions of the nurses can best be summarized by some of their comments:

This is what nursing is really about . . . caring for the total person.

I receive so much more than I give.

Our bereavement volunteers have helped so much.

As a parish nurse, I can be creative, and I can make a difference.

Learning about wholistic health has helped me in my personal life and also in my other nursing job.

I have gotten to know some of the church members so well and that has been a source of joy for me.

I think our parish health ministry has created more fellowship at our church.

After I did the program on Adult Children of Alcoholics, two members called me.

Pastor told me that the new family that joined the church said that our parish health ministry was a factor in their decision.

My own faith and prayer life has grown since I have been a parish nurse.

The frustrations of the nurses in Northwest Iowa are similar to other parish nurses (McDermott and Mullins, 1989). The main frustrations are lack of time, money and resources. Another frustration which has occurred concerns the lack of understanding of the parish nurse role. Some church members and pastors wanted some of the nurses to focus on physical nursing care. For instance, one nurse was requested to give the immunizations for the youth group, and another nurse was asked to perform venipunctures for a member's insurance requirement. The nurses declined such requests, explained why, and referred them to the appropriate person/agency. However, the nurses agree that the satisfactions outweigh the frustrations.

Special Considerations of
Rural Parish Nurses
and Networks

By describing the parish nurses in rural Northwest Iowa, I hope several facts are evident. First, it is important to determine what model of parish nursing is workable. Certainly, I wish all parish nurses were salaried; however, that is a barrier in the rural area. A description may help. For example, a 250-member church with 40% elderly with many on fixed incomes relies heavily on members' giving their time and talents. Janitors, choir directors, church treasurers and others are not paid for their services. Another aspect is the difficulty of obtaining start-up money for a paid coordinator, continuing education sessions, stipend money and resources for the nurses.

Also, the description of the nurses' activities illustrates that they are doing similar types of services . . . simply because human needs are similar wherever people live. Sometimes the rural area is idealized as peaceful and serene, with fewer problems than urban areas. In reality, the rural areas have as many stressors as urban areas.

However, the volunteer nurses do have narrower parameters of activities because of the time constraint. So, it is important that other members of the congregation are utilized in enhancing and developing health and healing programs. As a volunteer, the parish nurse needs support and guidance to avoid burn-out, as well as help in prioritizing her activities. Thus, a "buddy system" or a parish nurse coordinator who can provide support and educational direction is important.

In small towns, there is often a lack of access to health education resources. For example, some towns do not have a library, and, if they do, the library has limited resources.

Developed health education resources such as films and videos, are not readily accessible. Also, small congregations and towns may not have audiovisual equipment.

Another special consideration in the rural area is communication with other health and social professionals. In order to avoid misunderstandings, rural nurses always contact the local community health nurse to inform her about the parish nurse role, emphasizing the collaboration and referral aspects between them. Also, many rural parish nurses contact the local physicians as well to discuss their role and activities.

The nurses in this network are dispersed over 9,000 square miles. In addition, many of the nurses are employed in other areas of nursing. Therefore, scheduling the educational and support meetings for the parish nurses is a challenge. I have found that late afternoon or early evening works best. Also, all educational sessions are videotaped so the nurses who are unable to attend can view the tapes.

Record-keeping is another area that requires special consideration in our network. The nurses use forms which require minimal time to complete. The key words in our network regarding documentation are SIMPLICITY and ACCURACY. This facilitates maintaining a priority on the delivery of services. For example, the activity form is mainly a checklist and client record forms are flow sheets.

There are benefits or advantages in the rural area. The most obvious one is that many nurses were already doing "informal parish nursing" in their churches and communities. Also, in small towns, the church and church activities are often an important influence on individuals and the community, as well as provide the main source of social events. Also, the nurses in the project already had the trust and acceptance of their members, because they had known the nurse for years.

Conclusion

In our network, I use HEALTH as an acronym to remind us of our wholistic roles:

H - Health counselor
E - Educator
A - Advocate
L - Liaison to community
T - Teacher of volunteers
H - Healing

Parish nurses functioning in different models and in different demographical areas still have the same goals and purposes. They respond to the health needs of their church members and community as well as provide a valuable addition to the ministry of the church.

It has been and continues to be a joy to work with the parish nurses in Northwest Iowa. I dedicate this chapter to their caring, wholistic spirit.

Acknowledgement

I would like to thank Augsburg-Fortress Publishing, Inc. Portions of this chapter are reprinted with permission from a chapter I authored for the book The Parish Nurse by Granger Westberg.

Reference List

Magan, G., & Haught, E. (1987). Well-being and the Elderly: A holistic view. Washington, D.C.: American Association of Homes for the Aging.

McDermott, M.A., & Mullins, E. (1989, Winter). Profile of a young movement. Journal of Christian Nursing.

Miller, J. (1987). Wellness programs through the church: Available alternatives for health education. Health Values, 11(5). pp. 3-6.

8

ADJUSTMENTS, MYTHS AND REALITIES OF PARISH NURSING

Anne Marie Djupe

As one enters into the role of parish nursing, there is a time of adjustment and reality orientation. This is similar to the stages which Schmalenberg and Kramer (1979) described in their book on reality shock. The stages described herein are purely anecdotal from my interactions with parish nurses for five years. I include these observations because they may be helpful to new parish nurses.

These observations are particularly directed at the new parish nurse in a congregation which is also beginning in the program. There are many adjustments to be made by a variety of people, from the pastor to the congregational members. When a new nurse is hired to replace a parish nurse she may also feel much of this uneasiness even though the church staff and congregation may have a better understanding of the role and commitment to the program.

STAGE I: "Who am I, and what do I do?" This question can seem overwhelming in the beginning days to weeks. The nurse finds herself suddenly alone in an office in the church and wonders where to begin. Particularly, if the nurse is new to the congregation, she may feel very isolated. Most likely in any other nursing positions she has had very clear expectations with a very defined role. If the church is beginning in the program also, she may feel that they are un-sure what to expect of a parish nurse. She must educate not only the congregation but also the staff. She may feel even uncomfortable when she hears other experienced parish nurses talk about all of the things they are doing. She may also find it difficult to explain the role before she has had the opportunity to experience it.

The new parish nurse needs to be supported during this time and helped to recognize the importance of this time for building relationships and data gathering.

STAGE II: "When do I stop?" Suddenly, the programs begin, the requests come in and there are shut-ins to visit and meetings to attend. At about this point (3-6 months) the nurse begins to wonder why she took this job. This can be a time of reevaluation and questioning regarding the role, her strengths and abilities and the challenge of developing a bal-ance. Her family may start complaining about the many hours and she wonders how she will ever be able to meet all of the needs.

STAGE III: "I think I know what I'm doing now, but will the program continue?" Towards the end of the first year, the nurses begin to feel quite comfortable in their role. They have interacted with many members of the con-gregation and feel good about their accomplishments. How-ever, as the end of the first year rolls around, there is the time of evaluation and anxiety for the nurse. This issue is particularly emphasized for salaried nurses as the church de-termines its budget for the coming year. If the church is tak-ing on more of the salary of the nurse, they may be critical and question the impact of the program. The nurse may feel concern as to whether she has been effective in her role and how well the congregation and staff understand and recog-nize the value of such a program. Generally, the nurses are asked to report at the annual meetings of the church, which becomes a logical time for program evaluation. This issue emphasizes the need for regular communication which may be through monthly and annual reports. As one parishioner said, "This is a quiet and confidential ministry. Much of what the parish nurse does we will never know about." It is critical for the nurse to inform the congregation about her activities without breaching confidentiality.

STAGE IV: "I'm at peace with what I'm doing even though I don't know what the future will bring." There seems to be a time of resolution for the nurse. Even though she is in a new type of role with many questions and uncertainties, this is where she wants to be. That doesn't mean there aren't periods of discouragement and questioning, but overall, the nurse feels settled in the role. There also seems to be a shift in the nurse's implementation of the role. She seems to shift from program activities and very visible actions to more one-to-one counseling and referrals. She becomes much more involved in the concerns and needs of individuals and families. At this point, the parish nurse also tends to reach out more into the community by responding more to community needs and interacts even more with community programs and agencies.

Certainly, the first year is a time of adjustment and learning for the nurse as well as the church staff and congregation. As welcomed as the program may be, ongoing communication and evaluation are critical to the continuance of the program.

Myths and Realities

Along with the stages of reality shock, the parish nurse must also confront a number of myths which seem to surface and seem to be somewhat unique to this aspect of nursing. In order to continue in the role, these issues must be allowed to surface and confronted in a therapeutic and supportive manner.

Many of the parish nurses came from the fast-paced, high technical world of acute care nursing. They spent hectic shifts running from bedside to bedside, lifting, turning, monitoring machines, giving medications, IVs, feedings, and tubes everywhere. They would frequently leave their shift exhausted and wondering why they ever went into nursing in the first place and how they could keep up the pace as well as the physical strain.

Many of us went into nursing at the ripe age of 18 or 19 with very high ideals about what it meant to care, to be with people, to listen to their concerns, to answer their questions, and to calm their fears. By the time we graduated, we were ready to implement our technical skills as well as our caring skills. However, we quickly discovered the limitations and realities of working in this fast-paced, technical world.

One of the major reasons that nurses are drawn to the role of parish nurse is that this role gives them permission to be with people and to reclaim some of those ideals. Benner and Wrubel (1989) define caring as "being connected, having things matter. Caring fuses thought, feeling, action, knowing, and being."

Because caring is relational, there are many possibilities and opportunities inherent in that type of involvement. However, we know that involvement can lead one to experience not only joy and fulfillment but also loss and pain.

In order to put this into a framework which describes some of these perspectives, I have chosen to call these statements "myths." That does not deny that they are based on some truth but may become absolutes and cause distress for the parish nurse. I describe them for the purpose of identifying and naming them in an effort to open up channels of communication and reality testing among parish nurses, their peers and co-workers.

I have been gathering these thoughts in my mind as I have listened to parish nurses. I must also add a personal note. Having grown up in a minister's family, I was keenly aware of issues which confront people in ministry and observed how these issues began to affect the nurses.

Myth #1: The Parish Nurse Has All The Answers

"You are a nurse, certainly you have read the latest about that new test for cancer. What do you think about flu immunization? Should I see a doctor for this pain? If so, which one?" The list of questions goes on and on. A parish nurse may be seen as the key medical consultant in the congregation who has the latest information on all subjects and for all age groups. The reality is, each nurse comes to this role with various experience and expertise. The new parish nurse may feel this burden. One nurse commented that she felt like she had to memorize the Taber's Medical Dictionary. It is important to recognize one's limitations and develop a network of clinical resources to obtain answers for the parishioners. In order to establish her credibility, she must provide sound advice and recommendations so it is important that she learn to say to people when she is unsure that she will be happy to find out and get back to them.

Myth #2: The Parish Nurse is the Perfect Model of Health

The parish nurses seem to struggle with this issue quite a great deal. If a parish nurse is teaching others about health and wellness, how could she personally experience physical or emotional illness. She may feel that she needs to be the proper weight, exercise daily, and eat a well-balanced, nutritious diet. She may also feel that she must always be able to handle her stress effectively and balance all the demands in her life effortlessly. Whereas these are certainly admirable goals for everyone, they must not be viewed as unnecessary burdens in fulfilling the role. I have heard parish nurses describe the inner struggle and guilt as they experienced illness. The parish nurse is a role model for health to the members of the congregation. However, that does not imply perfection. Health is a process and perfect health in the wholistic sense is not attainable here on earth. The parish nurse must come to a place of acceptance of her humanness and struggle, while also recognizing the opportunity and challenge to model healthy behaviors. It is an issue of maintaining balance and a realistic perspective in one's life.

Myth #3: The Parish Nurse's Family Always Behaves Properly

The parish nurse may begin to experience some of the feelings common to the clergy. One of those relates to the feeling of being "on stage" or the center of attention. This is particularly true for nurses working in their own congregation. Suddenly, the nurse and her family may be viewed in a different light. Just as the nurse herself may feel the need to always be healthy and whole, she may also have a new awareness of how the congregation is viewing her family. Certainly, if she is supporting and counseling others regarding their relationships and lifestyle, she may feel that her own family must be a model for others. Parishioners may become critical of the parish nurse's family just as they often have of the clergy's family. The pastor often feels that his family is a reflection of his faith and trust in God. The nurse may also begin to experience this and may feel particular stress when her own family goes through periods of disruption and disharmony. The nurse may feel additional pressure when difficulties do arise to handle them effectively. Certainly again, the issue of humanness arises.

Myth #4: The Parish Nurse Can't Be Friends With Members of the Congregation

The parish nurse may feel uneasy about special friendships in the congregation. The issues seem to center around confidentiality as well as feeling like she may be showing favoritism to some members in the congregation. This may especially be true for nurses who grew up in that particular congregation. She may either feel awkward about continuing friendships in the congregation or on the other end, feel she must be friends with everyone. It is analogous to the staff nurse moving up into a management role where now she must reassess her friendships and relationships in light of the new role. She may feel she can no longer look to congregational members for her main source of support and encouragement. This is why it is so important for parish nurses to form their own network and have support from each other as well as develop support systems with the parish and pastoral staff.

Myth #5: The Parish Nurse Helps Everyone Who Asks

The parish nurse is carving out a niche in a new role. She feels that she has to respond to needs as they arise. Before long, the needs begin to exceed her time and abilities. She then has to come to grips with her own limitations and learn when it is OK to say "No" and not feel guilty. This is where support is vital for the nurse. This is a common struggle for professionals in the helping professions and we need to help each other deal effectively with this issue. It is extremely helpful when members of the pastoral staff or health cabinet can support the parish nurse in prioritizing and limit-setting. This seems to be a critical issue which must be addressed in order for the nurse to continue in the role for any period of time without feeling frustrated and "burned out."

The parish nurse who has become very involved in her role may begin to hear people saying that they won't call her because she's ''too busy.'' One nurse heard a parishioner say that the nurse always has time for me but she doesn't have time for everyone. It may become somewhat of a status symbol to have ''your special nurse.'' This can become very manipulative and what was intentioned to be helpful and caring becomes unhelpful. It is important to listen to these comments and to understand their messages.

Myth #6: The Clergy Are Above Human Struggles

Over the years, the parish nurses have become a source of support for not only members of the congregation and the community, but also to the parish staff. This role can be extremely important as the pastoral staff may feel a lack of personal support. Clergy also struggle with many of the myths listed above. Whereas the nurse may feel very positive in this supportive role, it also may bring with it feelings of disappointment and disillusionment. The nurse may have grown up with the concept of the clergy as being ''special'' people who do not experience the same frustrations and struggles of others. It may be difficult to suddenly come face to face with the realities that the clergy share these same feelings and frustrations as others.

Myth #7: The Parish Nurse is on Call 24 Hours a Day

Each nurse must determine her own limitations within the role of parish nurse. Just as the minister may be called at any time during the day or night, so may the parish nurse and she must decide how she will handle the calls. She must decide her limitations and back-up systems which may include purchase of an answering machine. Otherwise, she may feel that she is unable to take vacations or personal time.

Time is a very precious commodity and the nurse must decide how it is to be utilized most effectively.

When the parish nurse is a member of the congregation in which she works, she may feel that she is never off duty. When she comes to the church to worship or participate in an activity, she is seen by the parishioners in her role as parish nurse. Just as with many clergy, they feel they must actually be away from the parish to have time for themselves, or have to worship elsewhere in order to fully participate in worship. The nurse needs to find ways to feel supported and spiritually nurtured.

Myth #8: The Parish Nurse is Accountable To Everyone

When there is a cooperative program between a health care institution and a congregation, the parish nurse may feel that she is accountable to the hospital, the pastoral staff, the health cabinet, and the congregation. This may feel very fragmented particularly when the lines of communication and authority are not clearly delineated. She may begin to feel expectations from many directions and wonder where her allegiance really belongs. This issue must be confronted and discussed as it arises and clarified whenever possible. It may be helpful for the health cabinet to designate one person as the contact person for the parish nurse. It is also important early on in the program to determine who will be evaluating the nurse herself as well as making decisions regarding the continuation of the program.

Myth #9: The Parish Nurse is a "Pseudo-Minister"

As the parish nurses develop their roles, they get involved in many pastoral activities such as participating in services, bringing communion to parishioners, and visiting the sick. It is an ongoing issue to maintain a balance between pastoral and nursing activities. The foundation of her nursing knowledge and practice must be an underlying theme in all of her activities. This is what makes the parish nurse role unique and must be preserved. As the role is developed, defined and evaluated in various settings, this issue must constantly be confronted and discussed. This is a new role for the congregation and the clergy and there are no simple answers or specific limitations to the role, so we must continue to define the role out of our experience. Initially, because the Lutheran General nurses were coming out of the medical model of health care delivery, we seemed to focus our educational sessions much more heavily on the pastoral dimension of the role. After a while, parishioners and pastors began to ask for more information about health-related issues. When the nurse stopped blood pressure screening, people asked that it be resumed. There has to be a balance. It is critical to the parish nurse role that nursing knowledge continue to be a foundation for practice.

Myth #10: The Parish Nurse is Always Happy

This myth again refers to the nurse feeling like she is always on stage and that she must always be "up." This is commonly expressed by the pastoral staff as well. One of the pastors said that he could never have a "bad day." He said it was difficult to find places where he could let down and truly be himself. This again reinforces the need for ongoing support and supervision where the parish nurse can discuss her feelings and get feedback. It is also important to discuss these feelings with the pastoral staff. If this issue is not addressed, it will eventually impact family members and other significant relationships.

Summary

These myths have some truth in them and provide a basis for open sharing between nurses and pastoral staff. As the nurse enters into the realm of ministry, she may begin to feel many of the same pressures as the pastors. Working in a role such as this often raises personal issues for the nurse and can become a strain on the nurse as well as her family and significant others. The first step in dealing with the issues is awareness, and this chapter has been developed for that purpose. If any of these myths resonate with you, take the opportunity to look further and find some constructive ways to deal with them. Remember that health is a lifelong process with ups and downs, struggles and triumphs. The parish nurse role provides a wonderful opportunity to share with others in this process as well as striving toward your own sense of health and wholeness.

Reference List

Benner, P., & Wrubel, J. (1989). The Primacy of Caring: Stress and Coping in Health and Illness. Menlo Park, CA.: Addison-Wesley Publishing Corporation.

Schmalenberg, C., & Kramer, M. (1979). Coping with reality shock: The voice of experience. Wakefield, MA.: Nursing Resources.

Section III

PARISH NURSING:
ISSUES AND CONCERNS FOR THE DEVELOPING PRACTICE

9

ASSESSMENT: YOURSELF, THE CONGREGATION AND THE COMMUNITY

Anne Marie Djupe

*W*hen nurses make the transition from traditional nursing roles into the role of parish nurse, there are many adjustments that have to be made. Most traditional roles are very structured with a very defined role description. Among the attractions of the parish nurse role is the independence and autonomy to create a role in a nontraditional setting such as the church. Another aspect which is very important to parish nurses is the ability to practice nursing within a wholistic framework.

The educational process is ongoing and continuing. In this chapter, several components of the assessment process will be discussed: assessment of self, congregation and community.

When a nurse enters the role of parish nurse, she often feels much pressure to start organizing programs, screening blood pressures, and performing in other activities. However important that may seem, the initial phase is a critical time for assessment and relationship-building. It is a time for gathering of information about the setting, the environment and listening to the needs of others. It is a critical time for planning and developing a referral network.

Assessment of Self:
Knowledge and Strengths

The first major component is the assessment of one's knowledge and personal strengths. It is important to determine one's strengths and limitations early on in the role. A parish nurse cannot meet the needs of everyone and she needs to recognize this from the very beginning. When considering the major roles of the parish nurse, there is considerable difference in implementation by individual nurses. Some of the nurses in the program are more effective with one to one interactions and are quite uncomfortable in front of large groups. Other nurses like to teach health education classes, whereas others are outstanding at gathering support of volunteers for various causes. Nurses have experience in many different aspects of nursing such as the nursing care of adults and may be uncomfortable with questions about care of infants and children. Others may have experience in psychiatric nursing and may not know the latest information about blood glucose monitoring or treatment for people with diabetes. This is why a support network of resource people is so very important. Each nurse comes with unique strengths, experience and knowledge. She must utilize them to their fullest as well as recognizing when she must turn to others for assistance. A role such as this offers many opportunities for personal growth and development.

Spirituality

Another major element of the assessment process is the evaluation of one's spirituality. An ongoing issue for the nurses is discussion regarding their spiritual life and how they can integrate this into their practice. It is important for the nurses to determine how they can share their faith in a way that is comfortable for them as well as acceptable for their clients. It is very helpful for the parish nurse to process this with other parish nurses and a pastor or chaplain on a regular basis.

Time

Even though the parish nurse may have a contract for a certain number of hours per week, the issue of time must continuously be monitored. Nurses traditionally have had difficulty setting limits and recognizing their limitations, which may be intensified in this role. It is impossible to respond to all the needs which may be expressed. The parish nurse must make some important decisions regarding her availability, such as whether or not she will give out her home phone number or have an answering machine at home. It takes a delicate balance to be available and responsive to others while maintaining one's personal time as well as having time for one's family.

Assessment of the Church and the Congregation

Even if a parish nurse has ''grown up'' in the congregation in which she is now serving, it is helpful to step back and look at the church and its setting from different perspectives. Just as a nurse needs to find her way around a different hospital, a parish nurse also needs to know her new setting.

The Church Structure

A careful tour through the church building(s) tells one a great deal about the congregation. Does this church emphasize their program for the youth? How many Sunday School rooms are there? Is there a program for teens? Is there a weekday program for children? What about young mothers? Are there support programs for them? What kind of posters and flyers are around the church? What arrangements are made for the handicapped? Are there ramps and washrooms that are wheelchair accessible? What about the elderly? Are there large-print Bibles and hymn books available? Are there hearing devices available? Are entrances accessible for the elderly? Is there transportation available for the elderly who can no longer drive? Is there a library? What kind of books are in it? Is the temperature of the building comfortable (especially for children and older adults)? Is there a large room for groups and educational events? Is there a room with privacy for the parish nurse to meet with individuals or small groups?

Church Membership and Budget

It is important to know the membership of the congregation; what is the breakdown of age groups, and how many families are served. Are there particular ethnic groups which predominate in the church? What is the level of involvement of various age groups in the decisionmaking of the congregation? What is the level of involvement of various age groups in the activities? How many people are homebound or in nursing homes? What services are available for child care during programs and activities? What is the income level of the membership and what is the annual budget? Does the church meet its budget annually? Where will the parish nurse fit into the budget and what funds will be available for speakers and supplies?

Current Services and Staff

The parish nurse must have a good knowledge about the programs and services being offered in the church and the staff members currently available to provide those services. She can begin to ask how the staff feels about those services and whether some of the needs they recognize could be met by the parish nurse. What age groups seem to be underserved? What are the kinds of medically related concerns in the congregation? Which hospital do most most members go to and what is the system for visitation of the sick? How are crises handled and by whom? What is the system of referral and back-up among the various staff members?

Philosophy and Mission

The nurse needs to understand how the congregation views itself. Is this a church aimed at caring for its own members or is its focus on outreach? If it is on outreach, how is that accomplished? Are there programs for the community, foreign missions, the underserved? What does the church say about itself in their ads or signs such as "friendly" "caring" and "community?" These views can also be found in the written documents of the church and its denomination. It is helpful to learn about the history of the congregation. Who were the "founding fathers"? Are any family members or those pioneers still in the church? What are the denomination beliefs? How does the church relate to the denomination?

A parish nurse program needs to be congruent with the mission and philosophy of the church. This takes careful planning and education of the congregation. A tool may be utilized to obtain some initial feedback as to how parishioners view such a program and how they envision that they might utilize the services of a parish nurse (Appendix A).

Organizational Structure

The nurse needs to know the decisionmaking process in the church. How are the boards structured and how much autonomy does the pastor have? To whom does the nurse report and by whom will she be evaluated? Who are the main leaders and what style of leadership exists in the congregation?

Assessing Educational Needs

After the parish nurse has a good understanding of the congregation and the building in which she will work, she can begin to sort out some priorities. However, further analysis is necessary. In order to plan programs and activities, the parish nurse must be aware of the particular needs of that congregation and community. A "need" is defined as "a condition or situation in which something necessary or desirable is required or wanted" (Bell, 1978). A need may be perceived by an individual or by others. The nurse must recognize that needs are not fixed—they are constantly changing so an ongoing assessment process is needed. There are two issues which frequently arise. First, the nurse may have a long-range plan all arranged when an immediate problem arises. Such was the case when a parish nurse became aware of students from her congregation using steroids. Along with individual counseling and referral, there was also a need to present a program for all the youth on the dangers of steroid use. That's where the nurse must be adaptable and flexible. The second issue is more complex. Frequently, the parish nurse may be asked to organize classes on communication or conflict. She must determine what really is the issue she has been asked to address. Is this really an educational need, or is it a way to avoid a deeper issue of relationships? She must determine the issues, the people involved and the best method to address the issue.

There are three sources of data for determining needs: the individuals, the congregation, and the community. The most common method of needs assessment is the use of a questionnaire or survey. There is no magic number of people you need to survey to obtain adequate data. However, even in a very small congregation, at least eight to ten is a good beginning. It is very helpful to represent as many congregants as is possible. Whereas surveys can be useful, it is important to think beyond them and consider a number of other very useful options. Some of the data-gathering options are described (Bell, 1978).

Checklists or Surveys

Checklists or surveys are quick and easy to answer. When devising a checklist, it is recommended to use a

5-point Likert scale for better evaluation of trends. Print must be clear and large for the older adults. Consider the age group being surveyed. Different approaches may be necessary for different groups. If the surveys are being mailed out, response may be very low (1%-2%), so consider conducting the survey during a service or a program and collecting them during or at the conclusion of the service. If open-ended questions are included, make them brief and understandable. In other words, clearly define what you want to know. One word of caution: don't put more on a survey than you are able or willing to deliver.

In developing assessment tools, it is critical to define the topics as clearly as possible with various age groups in mind (Appendixes B, C, D). The tool should be easy to answer as well as easy to tally. It is also important to give the participants feedback regarding the results of the survey which builds trust and fosters participation for future planning.

Advisory Group Input

An advisory group, such as a health cabinet, can be a good source of information about the needs of the congregation. However, it is important that they be a group that represents a broad age range and key target audience groups. This can be particularly helpful in the ongoing assessment and planning process. They can be the key link to the congregation.

Examination of Role or Job Descriptions

Consider the special volunteer roles in the congregation and what training they might need to fulfill their role. Examples are first-aid training for ushers and Sunday School teachers and listening skills for Visitors or Ministers to the Sick.

Reports, Minutes and Newsletters

Written materials, such as minutes of meetings, annual reports and newsletters, can be valuable sources of identifying health-related concerns for that particular congregation. For example, there may be a prayer list for people who are hospitalized or shut-ins.

Personal Interviews

Personal interviews can be particularly effective with older adults and teens. Even though this technique can be time-consuming, it is an opportunity to develop relationships as well as identify which aspect of a topic would be most helpful.

Telephone Surveys

Telephone surveys can be particularly effective with adolescents or young adults. However, they can be very time-consuming so the survey must be very succinct and the items clearly delineated.

Spontaneous Suggestions

Suggestions and unsolicited ideas will come from members of the congregation once the parish nurse is established in her position. This frequently happens spontaneously in informal settings such as the coffee hour. It is important for the nurse to make the person feel that their suggestion is valued while also trying to gather specific information about the topic. For example, ''what is it about aging that you would like to know more about?'' It is important to then test the topic suggestion with others to see if this topic would represent a large segment of the congregation.

Ongoing Program Reassessment

Reassessment upon completion of a program is an ongoing process. Members of a congregation may not be used to formal evaluation tools. Consequently, the nurse must be creative in obtaining feedback and suggestions for future programs. Parish nurses have planned general information programs on aging issues particularly aimed for caregivers. Upon completion of the program, they have had sign up sheets at the back of the room for a "Caregiver Support Group" or for further educational programs. There has been an excellent response to such programs and support groups have continued for some time after.

Community Demographics and Resources

It is very important for the parish nurse to know the community. She needs to be aware of the demographics and the geographic area which her congregation serves. She needs to be aware of community agencies which serve the area and programs already in existence. It can be very helpful to visit many of these agencies in order to build relationships as well as to introduce the parish nurse role to them. Through these relationships, the nurse may determine that there are programs which could be co-sponsored. The nurse may also advertise community programs in the newsletter or bulletin. It is critical to build a network of support agencies to whom she can refer clients and who in turn will refer back to her.

Analysis of community literature can be helpful in several ways. First, one can determine the types of health-related needs in the community. Second, it can help to identify leaders in the community and third, describe the key political and health related issues. The parish nurse may also identify people who might be speakers and resource people for programs through community literature.

Analysis of national health trends is critical for the parish nurse. She must be aware of new information being communicated to the public through the media, particularly new testing and screening recommendations. The nurse may be asked to interpret and explain such things as "good and bad cholesterol" as well as dietary recommendations. The guidelines for annual health screening procedures such as physicals, mammograms and pap smears are constantly changing and the nurse needs to be aware of these recommendations. Certainly, as previously stated, the nurse cannot be aware of all of this information; therefore, it is extremely important for her to have links to clinical resources.

Program Planning

After the data have been collected, it must be summarized and prioritized in order to begin planning. The data can be ranked into categories of highest priority to low priority. It is extremely important to give feedback to those who participated in the survey. A summary can be placed in the church newsletter or sent out to the congregants with a tentative plan.

Based on the input from the previously mentioned sources, careful planning is necessary. There are several critical steps in the initial planning process:

1. Determine the items of highest priority.

2. Determine the target audience; i.e., various age groups, males or females, or singles, couples, etc.

3. Clarify the items. What is it specifically that the participants want to know about the subject? The nurse may have to go back to people to clarify and narrow the topic.

4. Determine whether or not someone else either in the church or community is providing a similar program. For example, there have been many recent programs on AIDS. However, there are many aspects to a topic, so a parish nurse could present a program on the "Spiritual Response to AIDS." You might also consider co-sponsoring a program with a community group.

5. Determine who is available to assist you in the planning and implementation of the program.

Your health cabinet can be very helpful in collecting data for you as well as planning and carrying out the program. Your health cabinet can also be helpful in identifying speakers from the congregation and community.

6. Go ahead and plan the program or activity.

Timing

Another important component to planning programs is to identify days of the week and time of the day which would be most convenient for the participants. The elderly may be hesitant to come out in the evening regardless of their interest in the topic. This question should be included in whatever assessment technique is used.

Assessing the Success of the Program Activity

Just a special note here. Success cannot be measured by the numbers of people who attend these activities. It must be viewed from the perspective of those who did participate. Were their expectations met by the activity? Even if a very few came, was it beneficial for them? It can be helpful for you to review all aspects of the planning to see if you might have done something differently. First of all, determine what the usual number of people is that attend such activities. Then, consider such things as the topic, speaker, time of day, day of the week, time of the year, adequate publicity, weather, etc. When you have assessed these areas, you will have determined some recommendations for the next program. It is important to recognize that you won't always identify any major changes you could have made. Try to look for the positives and feel good about those who did attend.

Summary

Assessment is an ongoing process which goes hand-in-hand with evaluation. First, the parish nurse needs to assess her own strengths and limitations which provides a basis for growth and development in the role. Next, the parish nurse must continually be looking and listening for needs in the congregation and community. She may utilize informal as well as formal methods along with receiving input from the health cabinet and the pastoral staff. The ongoing communication between the parish nurse and the members of the pastoral staff and congregation is critical for her personal support and growth as well as to the sustenance of a successful and continuing program.

Reference

Bell, D. (1978, Sept/Oct). Assessing educational needs: Advantages and disadvantages of eighteen techniques. Nurse Educator.

Appendix A

Parish Nurse Program
Questionnaire

We at church _____
are interested in beginning a Parish Nurse Program. The Parish Nurse
functions as a health educator, personal health counselor, referral source,
coordinator of volunteers and support groups, and integrator of faith and
health. We would appreciate your input regarding the types of needs you
see in our church and ways in which the Parish Nurse might respond to
these needs.
We value your input. Thank-you.

Health and Wellness Committee

Please check all responses which apply in each question.

1. In what ways do you think a Parish Nurse might be helpful in our
   congregation?
   _____ Personal health counseling
   _____ Health education
   _____ Blood pressure screening
   _____ Visiting the sick
   _____ Training health volunteers
   _____ Health referrals
   _____ Other (please specify) _____

2. Would you seek out the Parish Nurse?
   _____ yes   _____ no
   If yes, please comment for what type of situations.
   _____
   _____
   _____

3. What kinds of "helping" ministries do you think need to be
   developed?
   _____ Support groups
   _____ Caregiver training
   _____ Meals for sick or homebound
   _____ Other (please describe) _____
   _____
   _____
   _____

Appendix B

Parish Nurse Program Topic Questionnaire
Teens and Pre-Teens

The Parish Nurse is a registered nurse on the pastoral staff of our church. She is interested in being available to all age groups for health related questions and concerns. As we plan for programs and activities for next year, we want to know which ones you would be interested in attending.

Please mark (x) program topics in which you would be interested:

Family Life & Relationships	Would you attend?			
	No	Maybe	Probably	Definitely
Dealing with Parents	☐	☐	☐	☐
Peers — when to say "No"	☐	☐	☐	☐
Babysitting	☐	☐	☐	☐
Healthy Living				
Healthy eating	☐	☐	☐	☐
Smoking/Substance Abuse	☐	☐	☐	☐
Activity/Exercise	☐	☐	☐	☐
Relaxation Techniques	☐	☐	☐	☐
Safety at school & play	☐	☐	☐	☐
Understanding				
Feelings: Happy/sad/mad	☐	☐	☐	☐
Sexuality	☐	☐	☐	☐
Steroid use	☐	☐	☐	☐
Health Related				
CPR	☐	☐	☐	☐
First Aid	☐	☐	☐	☐

What other topics would you be interested in?

_____

_____

_____

_____

Thank-you.

Appendix C

Parish Nurse Program Topic Questionnaire

We, the Health Cabinet and Parish Nurse, are planning program activities for next year. We appreciate your input and suggestions. We will report the results of the survey in the next newsletter. However, your individual response will remain confidential.

Please return your completed survey to the church office or to me.

Thank you
Anne Marie Djupe
Parish Nurse

I. Day of week and time

    1. When is the best time for you to attend health education programs?

        ____ Weekdays - daytime
        ____ Weekdays - evening
        ____ Sunday morning
        ____ Other (please specify)

II. Please mark (x) the program topics in which you are interested.

Healthy Living	Would you attend?			
	No	Maybe	Probably	Definitely
Outlook, health & Well-being	☐	☐	☐	☐
Healthy eating/nutrition	☐	☐	☐	☐
Stop smoking clinic	☐	☐	☐	☐
Substance/Alcohol Abuse	☐	☐	☐	☐
Activity/exercise	☐	☐	☐	☐
Stress management	☐	☐	☐	☐
Safety at home & play	☐	☐	☐	☐

Family Life	Would you attend?			
	No	Maybe	Probably	Definitely
Multi-generational relationships	☐	☐	☐	☐
Blended families	☐	☐	☐	☐
Single Parenting	☐	☐	☐	☐
Parenting issues Teens	☐	☐	☐	☐
Young children	☐	☐	☐	☐

Aging Issues

Midlife changes	☐	☐	☐	☐
Preparing for retirement	☐	☐	☐	☐
Living the retired life	☐	☐	☐	☐
Change and loss	☐	☐	☐	☐
Living Wills	☐	☐	☐	☐
Caregiving & Aging Parents/Relatives	☐	☐	☐	☐

Health Related Topics

Cancer Prevention	☐	☐	☐	☐
Hypertension/Heart Disease/Strokes	☐	☐	☐	☐
Diabetes	☐	☐	☐	☐
AIDS	☐	☐	☐	☐
Alzheimer's Disease	☐	☐	☐	☐

What other topics would you be interested in?

_____

_____

Optional Information:

Your age _____ Marital status _____

Male _____ Female _____

Feel free to attach any additional suggestions or comments.

Thank-you!!

Appendix D

Support Group Questionnaire

Are you interested in a series of meetings for support?   Circle One
     for self   yes   no
     for family   yes   no
     other   yes   no

Do you prefer meeting in the church or in homes?
    ___ church   ___ home

Are you interested in: (circle one)
    sharing concerns?
    a counseling focus?
    an educational focus?
    other: explain _____?

Ideally the program should meet: (circle one)
    once a week for six weeks
    every other week for six meetings
    once a month for six months

What concerns would you like addressed?

My needs will be met if (fill in the blank)

_____

_____

Thank-you!

Anne Rosenberg
Parish Nurse

10

ACCOUNTABILITY: A RATIONALE FOR DOCUMENTATION

Mary Ann McDermott

What first comes to your mind and heart when you hear the term "record-keeping?" A sense of frustration and hardly bearable tolerance for a necessary evil are common responses. I would like to share my own development in relation to valuing documentation over the last decade. When my faculty colleagues at Loyola University, Chicago, and I opened our nursing center in St. Ignatius Parish in 1981, we argued vehemently for several weeks about what kind of record-keeping we would do. Issues of format, appropriateness, legality, accessibility, confidentiality; even questioning at one point, necessity. Compromise yielded the minimum number and simplest of chart forms available, on which we and our senior BSN Community Health Nursing students would record parishioner visits. We refused to "reinvent the wheel."

I also remember, as the Director of the Center, balking every time I would be asked for a written report about the Nursing Center and its activities. I could enthusiastically give an impromptu speech about how things were going generally at the Center; however, I hated spending the time and energy to gather information related to statistics about specific numbers, ages and conditions of our patient population. I perceived these as artificial categories of clients being served.

What did it matter? I knew that things were going well and parishioners delighted in the care we were rendering. When asked for graphs that would depict percentages of time spent in a specific activity in proportion to some other part of our programming, i.e., elderly services in relation to school health teaching; or time spent on the telephone in behalf of patients in proportion to direct contact time with parishioners, my snappy and sometimes snippy response would be " . . . and just who wants to know?"

When in the third year of operation the inquirer was a foundation that was a potential source of funding, I started to shape up. The last straw came several years ago when a very scholarly faculty colleague requested permission to conduct a research project at the Center on the relationship of stated nursing diagnosis and the documented interventions. She explained that this study would be preliminary to a larger project to examine patient outcomes in a population served by a nurse-managed center.

I have been transformed into a believer! I have come to appreciate the need for documentation and the multiple purposes that it can serve. As unpopular as my message may be, I implore you to collect the data that says: "As a congregation, you have determined that a parish nurse can facilitate the 'wholistic approach' to health that you, as a faith community, profess. We are both aware that the term "wholistic health" is, for the most part, qualitative, somewhat ambiguous and difficult to quantify. As the parish nurse, I will share with you individually and/or as a congregation appropriate information that justifies my attempts in this position on the parish staff to facilitate your goals. I do make a contribution and as a responsible and accountable professional, I can and will provide documentation as to the process and outcomes of the efforts we make working together toward wholistic health. Indeed, with your assistance and the help of God, I do make a difference!"

Needs Assessment, Annual Reports
And Other Elusive Forms of Documentation

Although nurses, myself included, usually think of charting when they hear the word "documentation," I would first like to call your attention to a number of other tools and strategies to assist in demonstrating accountability to yourself, your profession, your employer (the parish and/or the hospital and/or other funding agencies) and the parishioners you serve.

How many of you, or some other parish staff member who might have preceded you, have conducted a needs assessment? This process might have provided the documentation necessary to have brought you on the parish staff; or you might have implemented such a study to determine exactly what the parish stated as their needs, in relation to nursing services. The needs assessment is documentation to which you can often refer in planning and evaluating the services you offer and, I believe, serves as the first step in accountability through documentation. These are the needs that you, together with the parish staff and congregation, have identified which will provide future direction for the program. I do not wish to debate perceived versus real needs or needs as opposed to wants or wishes; however, I do want to argue for needs assessments as an ongoing process rather than a one-time event. I also believe the parish nurse has the professional responsibility to facilitate the congregations' acknowledgement of unrecognized needs.

A documented communicated assessment leads easily to the next step of documentation, and that is a statement of philosophy or mission that provides the rationale for the parish nurse program. These statements should take into account what the parish believes about health, about nursing (including a statement about documentation, accountability and confidentiality), about the parishioners' responsibility for health behavior, about identified needs, and about the strengths and limitations of resources available (time, money, personnel). This philosophy need not be a long-term undertaking, but should represent input from a variety of sources. A health ministry cabinet or advisory committee is a likely author for such a document. Let me share ours with you. Remember that this is an academic as well as a parish program.

Loyola University Nursing Center and Home Care Service, a nurse managed center founded in 1981, is sponsored by the Niefhoff School of Nursing in cooperation with Ignatian Services, the social care component of St. Ignatius Parish. The Center reflects the purposes, values and Judeo-Christian philosophy of both institutions. Care is provided by undergraduate senior community health nursing students under the supervision of qualified registered nurse faculty. Graduate students in gerontological nursing are available for consultation in selected instances.

Together, faculty and students engage in the promotion of health, prevention of illness, and provision of care for the ill. We care for individuals and groups across the life span using knowledge, skills and compassion to facilitate the individual's movement toward health.

We believe that every individual is created by God and has the right to live and die with dignity.

We believe that health is a condition of wholeness arising from the interaction of physical, psychological, intellectual, societal and spiritual well being.

We are committed to the utilization of theory and research as a foundation for practice. We recognize the responsibility of the profession to disseminate findings pertaining to improvement of practice in a scholarly manner; however, individuals can be assured confidentiality of their personal records.

An individual's health need and our resources rather than insurance coverage, determines if the service can be provided. At this time, there is no standard fee for the service; however, our program's existence relies upon donations as a significant source of funding.

A clear philosophy/mission statement leads to the next step in documentation: the formulation of clear and measurable goals. These do not have to be fancy or numerous, but again should provide direction for planning programs and assisting you in limiting or expanding services. Although the mission and overall goals will probably stay somewhat constant until new input is elicited from an updated needs assessment, specific goals or objectives can vary month to month, during liturgical seasons, and certainly year to year. It is the clarity of these goals, however, that will provide you with the structure for evaluation: your own and your program's. They will provide the basis for the decision regarding what statistics you keep (Appendix A); provide the outline for your monthly reports and most certainly for your annual report (to the congregation, to the staff, to the hospital and/or other funding agencies, such as a foundation). It makes all of these tasks much simpler, although different publics are certainly interested in different specific outcomes. I should add that I believe all of the preceding reports are a means of documentation and should be viewed as such.

Questions related to the issue of confidentiality, at this point, are answered best in advance by deciding who is entitled to what information and how specific that information needs to be. Take, for example, the number and demographic data pertaining to alcoholism counseling referrals or direct service you are providing. You need to know this for the purposes of future programming; the pastor, and possibly the health cabinet, may need to know generally the magnitude of the problem. The congregation as a whole, however, may only need to know that such an area of need has been identified and documented and that services are being provided by the nurse to parishioners.

An annual, multifaceted program evaluation should be viewed as essential to ensuring the ongoing success of the parish nurse program. Satisfaction with the appropriateness, quantity and quality, availability and accessibility are essential components of the evaluation and cannot be over-emphasized (Appendix B). This input must be sought from both the congregation at large as well as from those directly receiving specific services. Individuals, families and groups served should be queried in a formal printed anonymous survey with a request for demographic data and responses that, for the most part, can be easily analyzed by hand or computer. The categories of questions should reflect the mission statement and might include items related to trusting and caring relationship; technical and professional skill; health teaching; use of other community resources and appropriateness of referrals; and wholistic health outcome measures. Open-ended questions that address perception of most and least helpful activities and a request for suggestions for future parish nurse program planning will provide the parishioner with a means of individualizing the evaluation.

I ask you to consider several other activities as a part of your concept of accountability through documentation. Keep an archival collection of your program development and activities. Keep "your story" in a box or file with or without anecdotal notes that reflect your personal insights about the development of this ministry. Minimally keep records of programs you put on, photographs, minutes of meetings, etc.

You may regard these as only memorabilia; however, I remind you that you are parish nurse pioneers. You are living/writing our history! You need to gather this information and hopefully these personal reflections, so that you can tell the story to others or let someone else tell your story, beyond the parish, to the community, to other nurses, to other health and pastoral care professionals. How much have you seen in the literature about parish nursing written by parish nurses? I have seen very little.

I urge you to tell your story in one more way. How many of you have developed a brochure for your programs incorporating philosophy and goals with specifics of service outlined? One that can be distributed to newcomers in the parish as part of the welcome wagon-type material? The brochure also communicates/documents what you are doing in your program that is similar to or different from other programs and can be used in approaching funding agencies and in easily answering questions about your program from outside inquirers.

Charting

Webster defines charting as "a map; a drawn or written guide." The second definition is "a systematic record of development or change." Isn't that what a chart really is or should/could be? Perhaps, however, your introduction to charting was similar to mine; a vocabulary list of Latin terms and voluminous abbreviations that were to be the tools for charting. If you are of a little later nursing education era, perhaps you had added to your introduction to charting, Weed's Problem Oriented Medical Record (1969) and learned to SOAP the chart. If you are from more recent times, you have added to your pocket PDR a copy of Chinn or somebody else's approved list of Nursing Diagnoses to use when charting. In the mid 80's you might have learned to use Siegrist's PIE (1985) or Lampee's Focus (1985) charting. Throughout

your nursing career, you may have learned to abhor charting. In parish nursing, you may have thought you had found
a haven: no medical record librarian on the parish staff will
summon you if all is not in order, no chart audits or quality
assurance committees to reprimand you if the ''right'' choice
of terminology for reimbursement purposes is not explicitly
stated.

However, I continue to be the bearer of bad tidings.
Documentation is a professional responsibility; it serves as a
means of accountability and assurance to the parishioner of
quality professional nursing service. In taking a paid position
as a parish nurse on a parish staff, you are different from the
voluntary ''do gooder'' nurse parishioner who in the past
may have rendered nursing services of high or questionable
quality on an intermittent, as-needed basis or as she/he was
available or interested in rendering them. We don't really
know what quality of service was rendered as we probably
have no documentation. The news may have been good or it
might be abominable, but we only have hearsay; only information based on many different perceptions of what the
volunteer parishioner was ''supposed'' to be doing.

Professional nursing is a covenant, a solemn agreement entered into with a client. The profession of nursing, as
defined by the American Nurses' Association (ANA) in their
1980 Nursing: A Social Policy Statement is: The diagnosis
and treatment of human responses to actual or potential
health problems. The documentation of that process is the
chart. In the Standards of Nursing Practice (1973), the first
standard provides an overall guideline for nursing documentation, regardless of setting or area of specialization: The collection of information about the health status of a patient is
systematic and continuous. The data are accessible, communicated and recorded.

Legally, at the minimum, the charting recorded by the parish nurse on an individual should contain an admission note, progress notes, flow sheets as appropriate and a discharge summary. Elements of the nursing process (assessment, planning, intervention and evaluation) should be reflected in the documentation. Even if not as detailed as a note in an acute care setting, all the mechanical elements of legal documentation apply to the parish nurses notes: legibility, grammar and spelling, correction of errors and the nurse's signature. The phrase "if it is not written, it was not done" should still be a reminder to each of us that this is a legal document and requires the inclusion of important observations and interventions (Appendix C).

If we are interested in maximizing wholistic health in a congregation, then it seems logical that the use of contracting as a strategy in order to maximize parishioner participation in health promotion, maintenance or restoration might be instituted. Contracts can serve as an individual's plan of care. Mutually agreed upon goals can be reassessed, revised or reprioritized as conditions warrant. Encouragement of responsibility for parishioner involvement in record-keeping might include a parish workshop on keeping one's own health record. The parish nurse could attempt to revive interest in the family Bible as an appropriate place to store family health records as well as a place to document other significant family events as done in the past; i.e., births, marriages, deaths.

Parish nurses I have met over the years enjoy their autonomy. In fact, that role characteristic is one of the primary satisfactions that parish nurses identified in a 1987 survey by McDermott and Mullins (1989) (McDermott, 1989). I ask you to give up some of that autonomy when it comes to selecting a chart format. Although you have a choice of format, I urge parish nurses who have ties with a common sponsoring hospital and/or are geographically clustered, to seriously consider a standardized format. This would be most helpful for consolidating and analyzing data trends, especially in relation to outcomes in the long term. The decision to standardize forms might well serve as a first step in gaining external funding for future program development on a regional or even national level (Appendixes A, B). The form indicated as Appendix D is particularly useful for recording the less formal, but still professional interaction. They can be printed on 4 x 6 or 5 x 8 index cards and carried in one's purse for easy accessibility.

Some type of standardization of chart format would also facilitate my next request. I urge groups of parish nurses in an area to initiate and formalize a chart audit process. In doing so, parish nurses will demonstrate their commitment to quality care and programs. Such a process might also provide insight into the continuing education programs needed by the parish nurse group; i.e., how a particular common problem might be more appropriately handled with a new and/or different intervention.

I mentioned earlier that a faculty colleague requested to do a research project, which turned out to be an intensive chart audit, to determine the relationship of stated nursing diagnosis and the documented interventions. The findings were interesting, informative and somewhat distressing. The documented nursing diagnoses seemed appropriate to our primarily elderly clientele's medical conditions. They included references to impaired mobility, decreased cardiac output, self-care deficits, skin integrity, comfort, tissue perfusion, nutrition, coping, social isolation and deferred home maintenance. However, appropriate interventions were not as well documented, except for assessments and monitoring activities. Although not missing entirely, the chart did not clearly demonstrate the frequency of occurrence and/or the relationship of nursing diagnosis to intervention; i.e., self care instructions, exploration and identification of psychosocial support, resources and referral. My very own colleague pointed out in her report her concern about lack of documented patient teaching regarding diet, medications, safety and stress management. The faculty teaching at the center "knew" they and the students they supervised did make these interventions with parishioners, but "it was not always written," therefore, one had only to assume "it was not always done." Some of us learn more slowly than others! As a result of the audit, our emphasis on accurate and relevant documentation increased. Discussion about documentation and some of its inherent problems (lack of time, lack of motivation) is also fostered through implementation of the chart audit process.

Parish nurses are often concerned with the confidentiality of the record. These are professional records and are subject to the same restrictions for access as would be true in any other health care agency. You should have a locked file for the official chart and the information contained therein shared only with other health care professionals or parish staff members as you and the recipient of service determine to be appropriate. Brill (1990) provides a brief, but excellent discussion of legality and confidentiality. Extraneous and/or personal notes about the client should be kept in a personal journal or notebook and, as such, are your own property and should not be kept with the official chart.

The future of parish nursing, as is the future of our profession, is highly dependent in many ways on the quality of our care. Our image is dependent not only on what we do, but in telling our story to the many publics who support us at all levels. Nurses have not done this story-telling as well as they should have in recent times . . . and they have plenty to tell about! One of the first sources of these stories is the documentation of the care we give, be it in the chart, in the annual report to the congregation, in the interim report for the funding agency, in the articles we write from our archival collection of anecdotes. When we engage in documentation, we might well think of the covenant we have entered into and view our writing as fulfilling the promise.

Parish nurses in my limited acquaintance also balk, as I once did, that what I do is hard to quantify. I do not deny this, but I ask you to keep trying. If we don't, not only parish nurses, but all nurses, will be out of a job. Those who hold the gold want to know what it is they are getting for their money. I am reminded of the story of the newly hired parish nurse who, in attending her first parish staff meeting, was asked what and how she was doing. The nurse explained that much of her time was taken up in parishioner interactions that were of a confidential nature and had very intangible outcomes, at least in the short term. At the end of the first month, she walked over to the rectory, feeling very good about the many accomplishments she had made. It was pay-day, and the parish secretary sorted through the staff paycheck envelopes for the nurse's name, located it and handed it to the new parish nurse. Once outside, she opened it to make sure all the deductions were accounted for correctly before driving to the bank to make the deposit. However, the check was nonexistent; only a note from the pastor that read: "Intangible rewards for intangible accomplishments! Jesus promised glorious rewards for such activity in the next life, but given my mortal limitations and those of my congregation, we like tangible results. Even Jesus did some healing that got documented so as to strengthen our faith in Him. Best you consider doing something similar to inspire our faith in you!"

Reference List

American Nurses' Association. (1980). Nursing: A social policy statement. Kansas City, MO: Author.

American Nurses' Association. (1973). Standards of nursing practice. Kansas City, MO.: Author.

Berni, R. & Redey, H. (1974). Problem-oriented medical record implementation. Allied Health Peer Review. St. Louis, MO: Mosby.

Brill, J. (1990). Handle medical records with care. The American Nurse, pp 47, 51.

Burke, L. J. & Murphy, J. (1988). Charting by exception. New York: Wiley.

Lampee, S. (1985). Focus charting: Streamlining documentation. Nurse Manager. 16(7), pp. 43-46.

McDermott, M.A. & Mullins, E. (1989). Profile of a Young Movement. Journal of Christian Nursing, 6(1), pp. 29-30.

McDermott, M.A. (1989). Addressing the health needs of congregations, Who are the nurses in churches? In National League for Nursing, Nursing Centers: Meeting the Demand for Quality Health Care, pp. 147-152. New York: NLN.

Siegrist, L.M., Dettor, R.E. & Stocks, B. (1985). The PIE System: Complete planning and documentation of nursing care. QRB 11(6), pp. 186-189.

Weed, L.L. (1969). Medical records, medical education and patient care. Cleveland: Case Western Reserve University Press.

Weeks, L.C. & Darrah, P. (1985). The documentation dilemma: A practical solution. Journal of Nursing Administration, 15(11), 22-27.

Appendix A

Name _____ Church _____ Month _____

PARISH NURSE MONTHLY ACTIVITY RECORD

Parish Nurse Individual Interaction

	Home	Hospital	Phone	Nursing H	Office	Informal
Health & Wellness						
Resource/referral						

Age _____ Child _____ Teen _____ Adult _____ Senior _____

	Parishnr	Non Prsh	Staff Member	Prof	Other	
Source of Referral to Parish Nurse						
	To Staff Member	To MD	Church Group	Comm Prgrm	Outside Comm.	Prvate Counslr · Other
Referrals made by Parish Nurse						

Parish Nurse Activities

	LGH	Church	Community
Meetings			
P - Pastor			
S - Staff			
PL - Planning			
CC - Client Consultation			
PN - Parish Nurse			
Education Program			
C - Coordination			
A - Attending			
P - Presenting			
W - Writing			
Support Groups			
C - Coordinating			
A - Attending			
P - Presenting			

TOTAL HOURS _____

Source: Lutheran General Hospital

Appendix A (continued)

Topics of Programs Presenter/Coordinator	No. in Attendance	Target Age Group

Meetings   No. of Times/Month

Appendix B

United Medical Center
Moline, IL
Response to Contact with
the Parish Nurse

1. Why did you contact the Parish Nurse?

_____ a. Personal health need

_____ b. Counseling

_____ c. Needed information about community agency

_____ d. Needed referral to a health professional (doctor, dentist, etc.)

_____ e. Support group

_____ f. Health education

_____ g. Assistance for someone else

_____ h. Parish Nurse contacted me

_____ i. Other

2. What kind of response did you have from the Parish Nurse? Check as many as apply to your experience.

_____ Caring _____ Rushed, hurried

_____ Efficient _____ Needs unmet

_____ Delayed _____ Competent

_____ Listened well

3. Were your needs met?

_____ Yes _____ No _____ Somewhat

4. What is your opinion of the Parish Nurse Program?

_____ a. Excellent, program needs to be continued

_____ b. Good program, should be continued

_____ c. Adequate but needs improvement

_____ d. Poor, needs unmet

_____ e. Not needed, discontinue program

5. Are you a member of the congregation?

_____ Yes _____ No

6. Comments and Suggestions

Date: _____ Name: _____

(optional)

Appendix C

Lutheran General Hospital
Client Record Form

Parish Nurse _____ Date of Interview _____

Physician _____ MD Phone _____

Hospital Affiliation _____

Name _____ Address as _____

Phone _____ Church _____

Address _____

Directions _____

Date of Birth _____ Marital Status _____ Occupation _____

Reason for Referral _____ By whom _____

Household Members _____

Family Members _____

_____

Notify In Case of Emergency _____

    Address _____

_____

    Telephone _____

Support System/Organization Involvement _____

Current Medications

_____   _____

_____   _____

_____   _____

_____   _____

_____   _____

_____   _____

_____   _____

Developed by Karin Johnson

Appendix C (continued)

Significant Illness

____ Diabetes _____   ____ Hypertension

____ Cancer _____   ____ Glaucoma

____ Heart Disease _____   ____ Seizures

____ Pulmonary _____   ____ Handicaps   _____

Allergies _____

Surgeries _____

____ Physical Concerns _____

____ Emotional Concerns _____

____ Spiritual Concerns _____

Lifestyle Risks

____ Smokes   ____ Obesity (30#)   ____ Nutritional Deficits

____ Drug/Alcohol Abuse: Self/Family _____

Stressors: ____ Family ____ Financial ____ Employment ____ Spiritual

Narrative _____

_____

_____

Presenting Problem

_____ Physical _____ Emotional _____ Spiritual _____ Social

Narrative_____

_____

_____

_____

Outcome

Referred _____

Follow up _____

Appendix D

Lutheran General Hospital
Parish Nurse Client Form

Date: _____

Name: _____ Age (approximate): _____

Address: _____ Phone: _____

Location: <u>I   C   H   HV   NH   P   PA</u>

Referred by: _____

Presenting Concerning: _____

_____

_____

_____

_____

_____

Outcome: _____

_____

_____

_____

_____

_____

I=Informal; C=Church; H=Hospital; HV=Home Visit; NH=Nursing Home;
P=Phone; PA=Pantry

11

SPIRITUAL CAREGIVING: A KEY COMPONENT OF PARISH NURSING

Marcia A. Schnorr

Nurses claim to be concerned about the whole person, but their emphasis often lies in the physical dimension of care. Nurses generally identify the psychological, social and spiritual dimensions as they describe humankind, but there is often a psychosocial and spiritual maze that may lead anywhere, or nowhere.

Many nurses hesitate to include spiritual care because "they don't want to push religion," "religion is the job of the minister," or "religion is too personal." Some nurses are uncomfortable discussing religion. Other nurses believe that they have considered the spiritual needs of their patients by inquiring about their religious preference upon admission. Parish nurses by their very nature may be more attuned to the religious needs of their "patients." Religious affiliation may be identified, and religious needs may be addressed, but what about spiritual care? Unlike other nurses, parish nurses not only can provide spiritual care, they should be spiritual caregivers.

Definitions

Spirituality and religion are words that are often used interchangeably, but they are not synonymous. Several writers have provided insights concerning the similarities and differences in these two concepts. For the purposes of this chapter, the following collective definitions will be used.

Spirituality is that life principle that pervades the the entire being, integrating and transcending all other dimensions of life. It gives meaning to life and death. It offers love and relatedness. It includes the need for forgiveness. It includes hope, trust and faith. It involves a belief in a supernatural or higher power (Bell, 1985; Conrad, 1985; Dettmore, 1985; Dickinson, 1975; Granstrom, 1985; Kennedy, 1984; Livingstone, 1977; McFarland & Wasli, 1986; Murray & Zentner, 1979; Stallwood & Stoll, 1975; Steiger & Lipson, 1985).

Religion, on the other hand, is an organized system of beliefs and practices. It is the spiritual application of the relationship between people and their God (Granstrom, 1985; Kennedy, 1984; Lewis, 1968; Livingstone, 1977; Murray & Zentner, 1979; Stallwood & Stoll, 1975).

Spirituality and religion are "related," but they are not identical. Religious care and spiritual care are also "related," but neither are they identical.

Review of the Literature

This brief literature review will consider two major themes. First, the indications for spiritual nursing care will be considered. Second, research related to spiritual nursing care will be presented.

Indications for Spiritual Nursing Care

Steiger and Lipson (1985) stated that many nurses are troubled regarding the extent to which they should intervene with the spiritual needs of patients. They warn that the nurse should, however, assess and support the spiritual dimension of the patient.

With all the emphasis on total patient care, Saylor (1977) and Young (1978) feared that spiritual care is often neglected. Patients do not bring their bodies to the hospital and leave their religious attitudes and spiritual needs at home.

The American Nurses' Association Congress for Nursing Practice (1980) developed the Social Policy Statement which says that nurses must concern themselves with anything that has the potential for affecting the health of an individual. Shannon (1971) and Soeken and Carson (1986) stated that the Code of Ethics of the International Council of Nurses requires that nurses be responsible for spiritual care and not just the more familiar roles of nursing.

Research Related to Spiritual Nursing Care

Lewis (1957) completed a thorough literature search relevant to the spiritual dimension of nursing care. She concluded that nurses lacked the necessary knowledge and skills — therefore, they neglected to provide spiritual care. This writer found little evidence in current literature to suggest that the situation is much different.

Hay and Anderson (1963) surveyed rehabilitation patients to determine how they perceived the spiritual nursing care they were receiving. The study concluded that nurses did not respond to any of their spiritual needs.

A study sponsored by the National Nurses' Christian Fellowship (1969) included interviews with 109 patients to determine their awareness and perception of spiritual needs. The study concluded that patients did not recognize spiritual care as the role of the nurse. The study further concluded, however, that many patients would appreciate it if nurses would address spiritual needs.

Chadwick (1973) questioned a random sample of hospital nurses to determine their awareness of spiritual needs in patients. While all of the nurses in the sample believed that patients have spiritual needs, 58% of these nurses believed that the spiritual needs (of patients) were not being met.

Kealey (1974) studied what patients perceive as their spiritual needs and whether nurses play a significant role in caring for these needs. The study concluded that 40% of the patients in the study were able to identify one or more spiritual needs, but these same patients were unsure of the role of the nurse in meeting spiritual needs. Kealey also questioned 24 nurses about their role in spiritual care. Half of the nurses felt unprepared to provide spiritual care.

Highfield and Cason (1983) completed a study to determine the awareness by nurses of spiritual concerns of patients. The results indicated that most of the nurses believed the spiritual to be part of psychosocial health.

Schnorr (1985) completed a study of nursing programs in the state of Illinois to determine if, and to what extent, spiritual care was included in the curricula. It was learned that all schools that responded to the questionnaire believed that there is a spiritual dimension to humankind. Nearly 56% of the responding schools equated the spiritual dimension with the psychosocial dimension of humankind, and less than 48% of the responding programs included the spiritual dimension in their curricula.

Research to Develop Theory of
Spiritual Nursing Care

In the past, most research related to spiritual nursing care was conducted in hospital settings. Most of these studies identified perceived spiritual needs and the inadequacy of nurses in recognizing and responding to these needs.

This writer completed research to develop a substantive theory in spiritual nursing care that may be helpful to nurses in any setting (Schnorr, 1988). This study used the principles of grounded theory methodology, a method that is especially appropriate for applied professional fields such as nursing.

For this study, the unstructured interview was used to collect data. Although there was no structured interview schedule, a guideline was used that included demographic questions and questions related to the research questions.

Health care providers and health care recipients were asked to recommend registered nurses who: 1) were involved in direct patient care; 2) include spirituality in their nursing care; and 3) do not equate spiritual care with proselytizing. Nurses who were recommended to this researcher were invited to participate in voluntary, confidential interviews, and interviewing continued until theoretical saturation was reached (no new information discovered).

The final research sample included 46 registered nurses, representing 12 states, 1 territory, and 2 foreign countries. The sample included nurses with varied sources of paid or voluntary practice and diverse areas of practice and specialty areas. The sample included nurses from each of the three basic educational programs that qualify one to write the licensure examination for a registered nurse. The nurses in the sample had from 1 year to 42 years of nursing experience.

Although the nurses were not asked about their religious affiliation, 44 of them identified themselves as Christian; the
other two nurses described themselves as "nontraditional."

Overview of the <u>CIRCLE</u> Model
of Spiritual Care

As a result of the data collection, the CIRCLE Model
of Spiritual Nursing Care was developed.

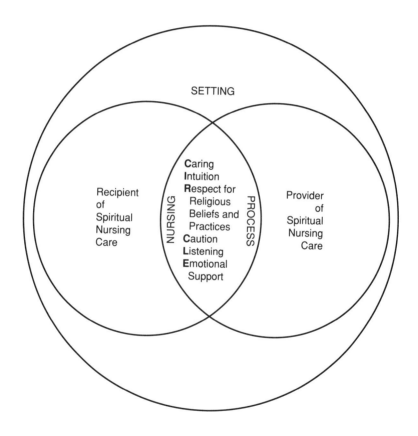

© Copyright, 1988. Schnorr

Setting

The nurses in this research sample had varied professional backgrounds, and they identified settings for spiritual nursing care that are just as varied. One of the interviews summarized, "Any situation can elicit a spiritual need." Spiritual care can, and should, be a part of nursing care in any setting.

Recipient of Spiritual Nursing Care

The "identified patient" is the most obvious recipient of spiritual nursing care, but the care could and should extend to the families, friends, other personnel, and nurses themselves. Everyone who is playing a significant role in the life and care of the "patient" has a potential need for spiritual care.

Provider of Spiritual Nursing Care

The provider of spiritual nursing care can be any nurse who has the interest, knowledge, skills, and commitment necessary to care for the whole person. This nurse is not limited to a particular setting or by a specific educational program. The provider is limited only by her personal philosophy of nursing care.

Nursing Process

Assessment. The three main "tools" identified for assessing spiritual needs are: (a) religious cues (b) emotional cues and (c) assessment guides.

The religious cues may be direct statements regarding a religious need, the use of religious jargon, religious comments, and/or a specific request. Religious cues, however, may be indirect — by referring to "the man upstairs," asking the "why me" question, or hiding the request in humor. The nurse may also pick up on a religious cue from items in the environment (e.g. religious literature, religious works of art, jewelry, artifacts, etc.).

Emotional cues are often the first indication of a spiritual need. The patient may seem depressed, worried, guilty, hopeless, grief-stricken, angry or ashamed. Persons who are experiencing a loss, including a loss of self, generally are experiencing a spiritual need.

Assessment guides are helpful in specifically addressing the spiritual dimension. Unfortunately, few nursing assessment guides provide more than a cursory glance at the spiritual dimension. Stoll (1979) developed an assessment guide that is specific to the spiritual dimension of humankind. A "Family/Individualized Health Survey" is available from the Social Ministry Services of the Lutheran Church Missouri Synod (St. Louis, MO) and addresses the whole person, including spiritual health issues. A "Parish Nurse Whole Person Inventory," which is available from the Parish Nurse Resource Center (Park Ridge, IL), also includes a section specific to the spiritual dimension of health.

Planning and Intervention. The six specific concepts which are included in spiritual nursing care are: (a) caring, (b) intuition, (c) respect for religious beliefs and practices, (d) caution, (e) listening and (f) emotional support. The first letter of each of these concepts form the acronym, CIRCLE.

Caring is the foundation for any nursing care, and and spiritual care is no exception. Caring includes (a) demonstrating care and compassion, (b) possessing an attitude that cares and (c) caring enough to take/use the available time.

Nurses must demonstrate care and compassion — and not just say that they care. Nurses have consistently referred to "tender loving care" as an important part of nursing care. What the nurse does speaks much louder than the words that the nurse speaks. Nurses need to show that they care.

Nurses also have to genuinely have an attitude that cares. It is the caring attitude that gives meaning to the caring behaviors.

Nurses need to take/use the available time. It is not so much the amount of time that is available, because nurses are "always busy." It is taking advantage of the time that you have, rather than waste it on empty words and hurried routines. Spiritual care can be incorporated into the time spent doing other "basic cares."

Intuition, as simple as it may seem, may be valuable in spiritual nursing care. Intuition includes (a) possessing instinctive feelings, (b) acting on instinct and (c) sensing the unspoken message.

Nurses who give spiritual care often describe a "feeling," an "instinct," a "gut feeling," and/or a "hunch" that there is a spiritual need. These feelings, of course, are grounded in an awareness of the spiritual dimension, practical experience, and an openness to respond to the spiritual needs of people. These nurses stated that they "follow their hunches" and are generally right. Many times it is the unspoken message of the individual that reveals the spiritual need; nurses must learn to "read between the lines."

Respect for religious beliefs and practices includes (a) making appropriate referrals, (b) praying, (c) encouraging devotional activities, (d) providing for specific rites and sacraments and (e) offering religious conversation.

Referral can be an important part of spiritual nursing care. Referral, however, should not be done for the sole convenience of the nurse. Referral should be made at the proper time and to the proper person — as determined by the needs of the individual. Some persons prefer to talk to nurses because they are perceived to be less threatening than the clergyperson who "represents God" and, therefore, is more intimidating. Some persons may prefer to talk to the clergyperson because their concerns can only be relieved by "the authority." Other persons may find their spiritual needs met best by a specific family member, friend, or an individual who has had a similar experience.

The need for prayer must be recognized and respected. Nurses may pray for patients, nurses may pray with patients, and nurses may allow patients to pray for themselves. The decision about how to pray, when to pray, and what to pray for should not be made before some basic assessments have been made. Prayer, whether for, with or by the patient, must take into account the patient's need in order to be meaningful.

Nurses can encourage devotional activities such as reading, listening to inspirational music and attending worship services. Some individuals find private devotions meaningful; other individuals prefer to participate in group devotions. Nurses can encourage the person to participate in personal and group devotions, and/or nurses can offer to share a devotion with the individual (patient, family member, etc.).

Nurses should know the religious belief of their patients and the rites and sacraments practiced by that religion. It is important that the nurse be prepared to perform or make arrangements for appropriate sacraments or rites in case of emergency (e.g., baptism). Nurses also need to be aware of dietary regulations, significant medals or beads, and other religious practices that may be meaningful to the patient. When the caregiver has the same religious affiliation as the recipient of care, this happens almost automatically. However, when the caregiver and the recipient of care do not share the same religious beliefs, the nurse must address the religious needs of the recipient of care and not those of the caregiver.

Religious conversations can be quite informal and nonthreatening. These simple conversations, however, can be meaningful approaches to allowing the individual to sort out spiritual concerns.

Caution is an important concept in spiritual nursing care. Caution includes (a) declining to proselytize, (b) avoiding judgments and (c) giving choices.

Nurses should never push, manipulate or force religion onto their patients. Patients will ''choke'' if nurses try to ''cram religion down their throats.'' Nurses need to be natural and live their religion, not preach it.

Nurses should not judge their patients; judging will only result in antagonizing them and the nursing care will be less effective. It is the responsibility of the nurses to minister to the wholistic needs of the patients.

On the other hand, nurses should not hesitate to offer the patient spiritual care, including religious ministration. When nurses do not offer, patients are not given the choice, and spiritual needs are not met. If, however, the offer meets with resistance, it is the patient's right to have her other needs met without being forced to participate in spiritual and/or religious care.

Listening includes (a) making an effort to hear what the person feels and (b) encouraging the person to express feelings. Listening is the most important skill the nurse can use.

Listening includes more than hearing the words that are spoken. Listening includes feelings expressed; it includes the meaning these feelings have for the individual. Listening involves getting to know people; their interests; their supports; and their aspirations.

Nurses must not only listen; nurses must encourage their patients to express their feelings. Nurses need to support and encourage people to express their feelings; nurses also need to accept both the feeling expressed and the person who expressed them.

Emotional support provides the vital link between psychosocial and spiritual dimensions of care. Emotional support includes (a) working through feelings, (b) showing love and (c) touching.

Feelings that are repressed will re-emerge later, often presenting a greater threat. Feelings, including those related to spiritual distress, must be worked through.

Love and respect can and should be shown to all persons. At times, nurses need to be firm; this firmness, however, must not be devoid of love. Empathy, not sympathy, is an important component of nursing care. It is difficult, however, if not impossible, to demonstrate empathy without feeling love.

Touch is important. Touch says that you care enough ''to be one with the individual.'' Nurses touch in many of the basic cares provided, but nurses can do more.

A hug, a pat on the back, holding hands all convey a message that often evokes emotional and spiritual healing. The nurse must also respect the individual who indicates discomfort in being physically touched and discover alternate ways to ''touch'' that person.

Evaluation. Sometimes the result of spiritual nursing care may not be immediately known. At other times, however, a positive change can be identified. These changes may be relational, physical, emotional, intellectual and/or religious.

The following examples of implementation of the CIRCLE Model of spiritual care are taken from my practice as parish nurse.

Mr. Smith came to the blood pressure screening that is held after each worship service one Sunday a month. The initial blood pressure reading was 182/110. Mr. Smith returned three times that Sunday to have his blood pressure rechecked; each time it was essentially the same.

Although the ''reason'' for his visit was to have his blood pressure checked, I was also able to assess his emotional distress. Mr. Smith was worried. I knew that his father had died of a stroke some years ago. I also knew that Mr. Smith works hard on the job and with several church and community organizations. Lately he had been subjected to a number of stressors. Mr. Smith's blood pressure was not his only problem.

I **cared** about Mr. Smith and demonstrated this through my attitude, my presence, and time. My **intuition** told me that Mr. Smith was worried that he may have a stroke like his dad. I also suspected that he had some questions about the future. Mr. Smith and I are members of the same congregation, and I knew how important his religion is to him. I showed **respect for his religious beliefs and practices** by sharing religious conversation, referring to scripture, and encouraging him to continue in the sacraments and religious practices that he has found meaningful. I used **caution** and did not judge him in any way, nor did I assume that I really knew him and his spiritual resources. I **listened** to what he said and didn't say. I tuned in to the meaning and the feeling of his communications, verbal and nonverbal. I offered **emotional support** by my words, my Christian love, and the use of touch.

Don't think for a moment that I ignored the 182/110 blood pressure. I referred him to his physician for medical management. His pressure is now 132/84. Jesus was concerned for the whole person and so should be the parish nurse.

Early one morning, I received a phone call from Mrs. Everest, an elderly woman who lives alone. Mrs. Everest was near tears and said she needed to talk to me about a "spiritual matter." I got dressed and went to visit her in her apartment.

Mrs. Everest was upset because she had not felt well for the past couple of weeks. She had seen a doctor and was given some medication, but she still felt a "heaviness" in her chest. Mrs. Everest told me that her daughter and son-in-law are not interested in her and get upset when she calls the doctor. Mrs. Everest went on to say that she wishes that she would have died first. Her husband died some 25 years ago. Mrs. Everest has always been a devout Christian, but now she fears that her "prayers don't work any more." She expressed a concern that "something may happen in my sleep and nobody would know."

I demonstrated **caring** by taking the time to make the early morning visit and showing compassion. For some time, I had an **intuition** that Mrs. Everest felt alone; today she verified my hunch. I **respected the religious beliefs and practices** of Mrs. Everest by using some of the resources that she generally finds meaningful. I read Psalm 121 and we discussed how comforting it is to know that God is our help — and He never sleeps. We prayed. We shared religious conversation. At her request, I agreed to share her concerns with our pastor. I was **cautious** not to cast a judgment on Mrs. Everest or on her family. I **listened** to her concerns and offered **emotional support**. Before I left, I gave her a hug and told her when I would return.

Mrs. Everest told me she felt so much better after our visit. The "heaviness" was lifting. She decided that she probably did not need the doctor now, but she felt confident that she could call him if she felt a need. She also decided to contact her son in another state, because she "feels closer to him." She was looking forward to the broadcast of tomorrow's worship service.

The relationship between the patient and the nurse is often closer when the nursing interventions include the spiritual. Relationships between family members often improve when spiritual issues have been recognized and addressed. Spiritual care can result in mending relationships that have been weakened by conflict and strain between individuals.

Some nurses reported, in the data collection for the research which culminated in the CIRCLE Model, that they had patients who required less sedation or less analgesic after they received spiritual care. Other nurses reported that patients "seemed sicker" before their spiritual needs were recognized and included in the nursing care.

Spiritual care can have a calming effect and reduce patient anxiety. Patients, families and other recipients of care seem more relaxed when their spiritual needs are met. Spiritual care "takes the edge off"; people are less afraid.

Patients get a sense of peace and are better able to deal with things when their spiritual needs are met. They are better able to accept the situation and make "healthier" decisions. They are more settled — not plagued by so many questions that have no answer.

Individuals may maintain or regain meaning from their religion as a result of spiritual nursing care. There may be a sense of renewal, reaffirmation, and reconciliation with their God, their church, and their inner self.

Conclusions

Most nurses include the spiritual dimension when they list the dimensions of humankind. Many nurses, however, confuse spirituality and religion and, therefore, neglect spiritual care. Spiritual care, however, is more than mere religion. Spiritual care includes caring, intuition, respect for religious beliefs and practices, caution, listening, and emotional support.

Parish nurses, like other nurses, may have varying degrees of comfort in providing spiritual care. Unlike other nurses, parish nurses are in a setting which makes spiritual care an accepted component of their ministry. This provides unlimited opportunity for the parish nurse to be instrumental in refining her skills in spiritual care giving.

Reference List

American Nurses' Association Congress for Nursing Practice. (1980). Nursing: A social policy statement, Kansas City, MO: American Nurses Association.

Bell, H.K. (1985). The spiritual care component of Palliative care. Seminar Oncology, 12(4), 482-485.

Chadwick, R. (1973). Awareness and preparedness of nurses to meet spiritual needs. In S. Fish & J. A. Shelly (Eds.), Spiritual care: The nurse's role. Downers Grove, IL: InterVarsity Press, 167-168.

Conrad, N.L. (1985). Spiritual support for the dying. Nursing clinics of North America, 20, 515-426.

Dettmore, D. (1985). Nurses' conceptions and practices in the spiritual dimension of nursing. Unpublished doctoral dissertation, Columbia University, New York.

Dickinson, C. (1975). The search for spiritual meaning. American Journal of Nursing, 10, 1789-1791.

Granstrom, S.L. (1985). Spiritual nursing care for oncology patients. Topics in Clinical Nursing, 7(1), 39-45.

Hay, S.I. & Anderson, H.C. (1963). Are nurses meeting patients' needs? American Journal of Nursing, 63(12), 96-99.

Highfield, M. & Cason, C. (1983). Spiritual needs of patients: Are they recognized? Cancer Nursing, 6, 187-192.

Kealey, V. (1974). Patients perspectives on spiritual needs. Unpublished master's thesis, University of Missouri, Columbia.

Kennedy, R. (1984). The international dictionary of religion. New York: The Crossroads Publishing Company.

Lewis, J. (1957). A Resource Unit on Spiritual Aspects of Nursing for the Basic Nursing Curriculum of a Selected School of Nursing. Unpublished Masters Thesis, University of Washington, Seattle.

Reference List
(continued)

Lewis, J. (1968). The religions of the world made simple. Garden City, New York: Doubleday Inc.

Livingstone, E.A. (Ed.). (1977). The concise Oxford dictionary of the Christian church. Oxford: Oxford University Press.

McFarland, G. & Wasli, E. (1986). Nursing diagnosis and process in psychiatric mental health nursing. Philadelphia J.B. Lippincott Company.

Murray, R. & Zentner, J. (1979). Nursing concepts for health promotion. (2nd ed.). Englewood Cliffs, NJ: Prentice Hall.

National Nurses Christian Fellowship. (1969). Report of a project of patient intervention concerning spiritual needs. Madison, Wisconsin: Author. Mimeograph.

Parish Nurse Resource Center. (1989). Parish Nurse Whole Person Inventory. Park Ridge, IL: Author. Mimeograph.

Saylor, D. (1977). The spiritual self. Journal of Practical Nursing. 26. pp. 16-17, 30.

Schnorr, M.A. (1988). Spiritual Nursing Care: Theory and Curriculum Development. (Doctoral Dissertation, Northern Illinois University, 1988.) Dissertation Abstracts International.

Schnorr, M.A. (1985). The spiritual dimension: The philolsophies and curricula of professional nursing programs in Illinois. Unpublished graduate research paper, Northern Illinois University, DeKalb, IL.

Shannon, M. (1971). Spiritual needs on nursing responsibility. Inprint, 28(1), 23, 66-67.

Soeken, K.L. & Carson, V.T. (1986). Study measures nurses' attitudes about providing spiritual care. Health Progress, 67, 52-55.

Social Ministry Services, Lutheran Church Missouri Synod. Family/Individualized Health Survey. Saint Louis: Author. Mimeograph.

Reference List
(continued)

Stallwood, J. & Stoll, R. (1975). Spiritual dimension of nursing. In I. L. Beland & J. Y. Passos (Eds.), Clinical nursing, 3rd ed., New York: Macmillan Publishing Company, 1009-1096.

Steiger, N.J. & Lipson, T.G. (1985). Self-care nursing theory and Practice. Bowie, MD: Brady Communication Company, Inc.

Stoll, R. (1979). Guidelines for spiritual assessment. American Journal of Nursing, 79(9), 1574-1577.

Young, D.B. (1978). Spiritual dimensions of nursing practice., Nursing Lamp. 24(5). 3-4.

12

MINISTRY TO OURSELVES AND OTHERS: PROMOTING THE BALANCE

Phyllis Ann Solari-Twadell

*H*ippocrates, who is regarded as the father of modern medicine, said that disease is due to natural causes. He sought to determine the causes so as to prevent the disease. He identified the four fluid substances in the body: blood, phlegm, yellow bile and black bile. He derived that when these four humors were in proper proportions, a person is in health; when they get out of proportion and a person has more or less than he needs, he is sick. Hippocrates suggested the way to cure the sick person, then, is to help him restore the proper balance (Scherzer, 1984). A recent booklet from the Christian Medical Commission of the World Council of Churches elaborates on this theme of health and balance. "Health in some societies is seen to be determined by balance (harmony) and disease caused by lack of it. Harmony of body humours and functions of mind, soul and body, of relationships with the environment and other beings play an important part in maintaining health. These traditional societies view health as complete harmony within an individual, family, community and environment, and may thus be closer to a Christian view of health (wholeness) than that of Western Medicine" (Healing and Wholeness: The Churches' Role in Health, in press).

Rev. Walter Wietzke (1987) gives yet another under-standing of balance as it relates to health. In his Precis on Congregational Health Partnership, Rev. Wietzke emphasizes a phrase popularized by Martin Luther: "Curvatus in se," or "turned back in on one's self.

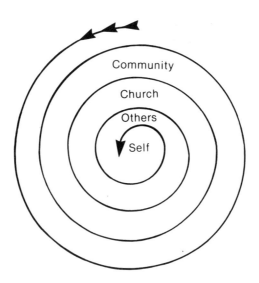

This diagram is reminiscent of a pocket watch. When it is wound too tightly, an impacted spring would not allow the watch to function. This construction limits self and im-pairs relationships with family, congregation and community. The opposite dynamic is an inside-out movement. This is where the self looks to others. This motion supports an en-dorsement of life for others and for self (Wietzke, 1987).

Pictorially, this diagram is meant to be dynamic, rep-resenting constant movement. Humans move back and forth between a narcissistic self-focus where God is moved to the perimeter of life to a more other-focused spirit-driven per-spective. The balance becomes very important. Self-reflection and introspection are important, but must be put into balance by a reaching out or "other-focused" perspective.

The nurse who chooses to accept the call to parish nursing tends to have a different perspective of self and community. For this person, wholeness is not a static balance of harmony, but is building and living in community with God, with people and with creation (Healing and Wholeness: The Churches' Role in Health, in press). Nursing is connected to a deep meaningfulness which is enhanced by religious or humanitarian values. There is an interweaving between what is being done and the ultimate meaning and purpose of life. There is, for this person, a sense of the effect of the self on the spirit of another. This awareness encourages the nurse to incorporate in the pattern of life, a time for personal reflection or prayer that seeks an intimate contact with God and implies contact with the self. This entails the ongoing process of self-emptying and an openness to sharing and receiving. There is a certainty of God's providential care which creates a trust that makes the nurse's own struggle and commitment more meaningful. It also entails a reaching out and sensitivity to the needs of others.

In Lane's article "The Care of the Human Spirit" (Lane, 1987), she discusses not only the works of the human spirit but also the activities of the human spirit. They are inward-turning, or the ability for introspection and reflection; surrendering, or the experience of letting go and letting be; committing, or the ability to attach or bond oneself to another; and struggling, which involves piecing together a number of life's elements to find meaning, cohesion and unity to life. The nurse, ministering to others through the role of parish nurse, is ultimately involved with this process. The nurse can recognize these activities of the human spirit in the people ministered to and facilitate their movement through the process. At the same time, the nurse is experiencing the same process for herself. A nurse who listens with the "third ear" for the spirit of the person served must make a purposeful effort to be replenished.

Professional Culture: Nursing

Each profession over the years of its existence has developed a professional culture. This professional culture is a system of knowledge, values, beliefs and truisms by which a specific professional group designs their own actions and interprets the behaviors of others (Spradley, 1990, p 5). A cultural truism is a belief accepted as unquestionably true by most members of a group. Cultural truisms are rarely called into question; when they are not, it is relatively easy to lose sight of why they are upheld (Aronson, 1984, p 102).

Nursing as a profession has, over the years, developed its own professional culture. Since early in their careers, nurses have been living with definitions of themselves and assigned cultural roles. It is important to understand how these dimensions of the professional culture inhibit or contribute to the "listening of the spirit."

Professional socialization is described by Jacox as the process by which a person acquires the knowledge, skills and sense of occupational identity and characteristics of a professional. The process involves the internalization of the values and norms of a professional group into one's own behavior and self-conception. It is important to recognize that professional socialization does not begin with entry into a professional school, but has its roots in the earlier experience of the person which results in the decision to join a particular occupational group (Cohen, 1981).

In internalizing the professional culture, there is an assuming of values, norms, cultural truisms, motivational attitudes and ethical standards held in common by other members of the profession. The professional culture exerts control over individual practitioners by reminding them of their common shared ideals.

Some of the images of nursing throughout the decades shed some light on the development of this professional culture.

In 1854-1919, nurses were pictured and described as "angels of mercy." Timeless hours were worked with the self-sacrificing women being able to move through the care of others with a gentle touch, soft word and unending patience. During the First World War era (1914-1918), nursing was marked with a more authoritarian, powerful image that signified a control over self and others. The 1920's gave way to a "Girl Friday image." The words which often described the nurse were "faithful, dependable, dependent, cooperative, suffering and subservient." The 1930 to 1945 era brought forth the nurse as brave, rational, decisive, humanistic, autonomous. This image was softened some from 1945-1965 with television's visual portrayal of nurses. The nurse was often characterized with motherly qualities such as sympathetic, maternal, nurturing, passive, expressive and domestic. More recently, through portrayal of characters such as "hot lips Houlihan" in the series "MASH," the nurse has taken on more of an object image, described as romantic, sensual, frivolous, promiscuous and irresponsible. All of these images at different times have had an impact on the development of the professional culture of nursing.

Nursing's Cultural Truisms

It is important, as time periods contributing to nursing's professional culture are reviewed, that some cultural truisms are highlighted. It is only by acknowledging them that efforts can be made to challenge and change those that may prohibit effective parish nursing practice.

Three aspects of the professional culture are the focus of this section. They are the understanding that the patient comes first; the denial of personal pain; and the sense of control and responsibility for another's well-being.

The Patient Comes First

This cultural truism is learned early; in fact, it may be one of the first. The patient to whom a nurse is assigned comes over and above any personal need. This sets the norm that lunch and breaks will be skipped. That even if the nurse feels ill, the expectation is to report to work on time. It provides early groundwork for the thinking that, as a nurse, I am different and must operate differently from others. Others need to take care of themselves, nurses don't. This thinking often makes it difficult for the nurse to ask for help; consequently, the learning is to do it by oneself. And somehow the nurse often does. This stance almost prohibits any acknowledgment of human limitation. It does not facilitate the process of introspection and learning of what I am as a child of God. It certainly requires no learning or trusting of others, but emphasizes more that the only person one can trust is one's self.

Personal Pain is to be Denied or "Stuffed"

In order to effectively carry through on the previous cultural truism, a second standard of denying one's own personal pain, disappointment, fear and losses is encouraged. The encouragement comes from a culture and system that functions most efficiently when an individual's skills and knowledge are learned without the emotionalism often associated with the expression of one's own internal conflicts and pain. It becomes easier in life as a whole to function on a level that continues to deny in one's personal life, any struggles and the accompanying emotional pain. So "stuffing of feelings" becomes the norm. In addition, the fullness of joy is stifled because the depth of pain cannot be acknowledged. This can become so dysfunctional for some that, at times, feelings cannot be identified at all.

Sense of Control and Responsibility
For the Well-Being of Others

Early in the nursing educational experience, it is learned that a patient's recovery can depend on how well the nurse performs. Inherent in this is a learned sense of control and responsibility for another's well-being. This cultural truism can produce problems when this becomes a practicing norm in all of life. The nurse can feel a sense of control and responsibility for her husband, children and other family members. This outlook on life can lead to a personal unmanageability and encourage the nurse to extend beyond her own human limitations. This sense of control does not leave much room for a spiritual perspective to be integral to one's life. The "listening for the spirit" of another is not acknowledged as the "all knowing" attitude of the nurse prevails in controlling the situation at hand.

Professional culture is multifaceted. The preceding cultural truisms are just a few of its dimensions. They are some of the most problematic, however, if they are prevalent in the primary functioning of the parish nurse.

The parish nurse position requires the ability to understand one's self and to be able to be introspective. The acceptance of human limitation is especially important if the parish nurse is to be able to care for self and effectively communicate that to others through modeling of Christian wellness.

The Life of Jesus
Role Model of Health and Balance

One of the best ways of moving toward a healthy balanced lifestyle is to read of how Jesus took care of himself as he carried the Word to others.

Jesus was human. He was a child, experienced adolescence and grew into manhood. He had feelings, and lived with human limitations. The following are a few of the things that contributed to his state of wholeness.

He Didn't Do It Alone

Jesus carefully selected people that He would teach to do His work when He was not there. This was extremely important. His ministry depended on it. If He had not carefully chosen and instructed His apostles once He was no longer here on earth, His ministry could have ended. He only lived 33 years. In that time he created a fellowship of believers who fostered forgiveness and restoration of healthy relationships in community. That community today is worldwide.

He Prepared Others To Help Him

His work was spent in teaching all, but He did take special time to ensure that those who would carry the Word were prepared to preach, teach and heal. Special time was spent in teaching and role modeling the behavior and skills needed to carry on the mission. Jesus left his family and moved out in the world, embracing the marginalized, the downtrodden and the imperfect. Through this He restored dignity and created community.

He Had a Close Group of Friends
Who Listened and Cared About Him

Jesus chose individuals whom He could rely on for support. These men and woman He chose followed Him wherever He directed. As they traveled one can picture the group sharing conversation and laughter. They weren't always able to comprehend the full scope of all that lay before them, but they understood the importance of the man Jesus. Jesus took the time to nurture them (Mark 9:33-37) and confront them (Mark 8:33-35).

He Exercised Regularly

This was a normal part of Jesus' life as He walked most places He went (Matthew 15:21). He did not need to seek out a routine as we do today. He usually walked with someone as He went about His work. His mission depended on His being in good physical condition. If He would abuse His body, that could affect His ability to fulfill His assignment from His Father.

He Loved

Jesus so loved His Father that His total life was focused on this work. Love was integral to Jesus' work. He reached out loving those whom others despised. Jesus' ultimate act of love was His death on the Cross. All need to experience love and give love which binds each in community with the other. Through community we learn to love and appreciate ourselves as children of God. God communicates to us through these relationships.

He Looked to Others for Support, But Not to Take Care of Him

There are many points in the story of Jesus' life where He relied on those close to Him for support. However, He never expected them to do what He needed to do Himself. Nor did He look to them to protect Him at times when He was required to do His Father's Will (Luke 22:48-53).

He Rested and Slept Regularly

Jesus did grow weary. The Gospels speak to the times when He rested (Mark 6:31). His human limitations were apparent and He did what He needed to do for Himself in order that He would be in the best position to serve His Father through serving His fellow men and women.

He Ate Healthfully

Jesus did not have a McDonald's or Wendy's along His route. His diet was simple. He ate what He needed to complete His Mission for His Father. He also saw that those who followed Him did not suffer from hunger (Matthew 14: 15-23).

He Was Honest

His life was not troubled with feelings of guilt or shame. He went about His Father's work in a most forthright manner. He did not have to worry about His responses for they were truthful. Often His honesty was contrary to what others expected (Luke 10:40-42), leaving them with something to ponder.

He Prayed Often

This is referred to often in the Bible (Matthew 14: 23-24 and Luke 11:1-3). This was an important time of communication between Jesus and His Father in heaven. He asked for courage, strength, and guidance to do His Father's Will as well as praying for those around Him who were ignorant of the message and were in pain.

He Practiced Solitude

This time of solitude was for His rest, reflection and clarification. He needed this time away from the distraction of the world and its people. Solitude gave Him time to refocus or become more clear about His mission (Luke 4:1-2).

He Was Open to All People

Throughout the Gospels Jesus is interacting with all people: the very sick, the poor, the wealthy, the farmer and the hypocrite. All became part of His mission and His work. No one is shunned or ignored (Luke 8:26-34).

He Trusted

His trust in His Father was without fault. He didn't always embrace what lay before Him, but He trusted that God, His Father, would give Him the grace, courage and fortitude to do the work. There was no whining or self-pity, but acceptance and surrender (Mark 14:36).

He Did God's Will

Jesus fulfilled the prophesies. He moved about doing His Father's work. He planted seeds and role-modeled to all how they could do the same. He spoke openly of His mission and encouraged His followers to join Him in community (Luke 5:4-10).

He Went About His Work in Spite of All Problems

Problems were acknowledged and often dealt with, but never did they draw Him away from the focus of His work. Problems did not weigh Him down or immobilize Him or cause Him to move off the course He was to follow (Mark 12:12-17).

Summary

Each brings different gifts to the role of parish nurse. All come with basic human limitations, experience in various nursing positions and often unique life experience. It is important to acknowledge the positive attributes of the nursing culture as well as those things that may be problematic.

Daily life brings with it stress, pain, anxiety, fear and sometimes loss, as well as love, laughter and companionship. Striving for a healthy balance in our lives gives an appreciation for the struggles of others. Regardless of what presents itself, the life of Jesus serves all well. As Jesus role-modeled for us, so we role-model for others. This is inherent in the role of parish nurse.

The laughing Jesus is an important image to keep in mind as each goes about their work. In closing, I would like to share with you the following poem by Rev. Dr. Walter Wietzke (1987, p. 6).

On Holy Carefreeness

I'm
tired of
those semi-religionists
with hang dog mein
moving achingly, faces scrunched with
pious despair, acting as though they
could redress all wrongs if those in
power would only capitulate and listen to them

Whence
comes this
arrogance that they
can rectify human error

Maybe
the Almighty
should recess and
let the wailers have
their day running the cosmos

But
He says
be of good-cheer

Only
the one
who has forsworn
the ambition to mold
every thing to one's own design
is free to laugh with God

Reference List

Aronson, E. (1984). The Social Animal (4th ed.). New York: W.H. Freeman and Company.

Cohen, H.A. (1981). The Nurses' Quest for a Professional Identity. Mills Park, CA: Addison Wesley Publishing Company.

Healing and Wholeness: The Churches' Role in Health (In press). A report on a Study by the Christian Medical Commission World Council of Churches, Geneva, Switzerland.

Lane, J. A. (1987, November-December). The care of the human spirit. Journal of Professional Nursing.

Scherzer, C. J. (1984). The Church and Healing, Chaplain of the Protestant Deaconess Hospital. Unpublished manuscript, Protestant Deaconess Hospital, Evansville.

Spradley, J.P. (1990). Conformity and conflict: Readings in cultural anthropology. (7th ed.). Glenview, IL: Scott, Foresman/Little Brown Higher Education.

Wietzke, W. (1987). Precis on Congregational Health Partnership. Unpublished manuscript.

13

CURRICULUM DEVELOPMENT FOR PARISH NURSING: AN EDUCATOR'S PERSPECTIVE

Norma R. Small

The evolution of a new professional nursing role such as parish nurse has predictable and observable phases: role identification and differentiation, role definition, standard-setting, curriculum development, and certification. Currently, consensus on the parish nurse role definition is being generated through publications and conferences, with the need to begin discussions on standards of practice. This is a very crucial phase for a new professional role since it will take the wisdom of Solomon to balance the "what it is" with the "what it could be" seasoned with professional, legal and ethical parameters to determine what the minimal standards of practice are and what educational preparation is necessary to meet these standards. The purpose of this chapter is to discuss curriculum development for the parish nurse. Given the lack of standards at this time, curriculum development will be addressed from a point of view of "what parish nursing could be," and maybe even better, "what parish nursing should be", in order to gain recognition as a nursing specialty and the legal accountability it needs to be valued in our society.

Identification of a new role develops from the "soil of social organization" (Erikson, 1950, p. 263). The "soil" that has fostered the germination of the parish nurse role has been the need of modern society for an integrated approach to health and healing in a health care system with soaring costs, a decrease in the overall health of the nation, and the absence of churches in the health care continuum. The increased health care costs result mainly from medical and technological advances which prevent death from acute illness and prolong the dying process, but which do little to promote healthy lifestyles that can prevent acute and chronic disease and injury. The key to improving health lies with the individual and his or her lifestyle choices and in society's responsibility to provide a safe and healthy environment. Nurses have historically been the leaders in health education and promotion and most Americans identify with a faith community. Thus, nurses are the best prepared health professional to take health into churches and promote their participation in the health care continuum.

Differentiation of the parish nurse role from that of a community health nurse located in a church is essential. If health promotion services are just add-on to the church's programming, a new role has not been developed. It is only when the theology of health and healing is integrated into the worship and ministry of the faith community that a unique role emerges. Health issues are best addressed within a faith community which ministers to the whole person through a wholistic definition of health as wholeness. A tenet of faith is the responsibility of each individual to be a "good steward of God's creation" and to be "his brother's keeper" in those areas which affect the abilities of others to live up to their health potential. Incorporating client's beliefs and religious practices into the definition of health and healing provides the differentiation necessary to qualify parish nursing as a new role requiring new knowledge and skills.

Role development is achieved through the assumption of norms, attitudes, standards of practice and competencies which are acquired through observation, education and socialization. The parish nurse movement can draw upon the experiences in the historical development of advanced nursing practice roles and especially that of the clinical nurse specialist (CNS). Dr. Hildegarde Peplau cited three reasons for initiating the clinical nurse specialist role: 1) increased knowledge germane to the field of specialization, 2) development of new technology and 3) response to a hitherto unrecognized public need or interest. New role development implies the attaining of a breadth and/or depth of knowledge beyond that required of existing roles in order to meet new organizational or societal expectations. The parish nurse movement is responding to these professional and sociological criteria by identifying and instituting a new advanced nursing practice role which meets the professional definition of clinical nurse specialist. While CNSs have a wide range of responsibilities, practice location and areas of specialization, the experience in defining the educational preparation and core curriculum can be applied to the preparation of the parish nurse.

To meet the immediate need to prepare parish nurses, the educational preparation is being defined more by participation and the sharing of experiences than by a curriculum based on a theoretical framework. As consensus is attained on the standards of practice and competencies expected of the role, the educational preparation necessary to meet these criteria will become evident. The standards of practice for the parish nurse should be broad enough in scope to encompass the diversity in size, location, composition and values of the variety of faith communities in which the parish nurse role may be implemented. On the other hand, in order to achieve clear role identity and acceptance within the professional and health care communities, the standards must be specific enough to define accountability to the consumers for specific services which warrant the investment of the time and of the churches' resources. Thus, the curriculum must be developed based on the basic criteria for the preparation of nurses in advanced nursing practice as identified for accreditation by the National League for Nursing (NLN).

Tyler (1970) outlined the basic principles of curriculum development: 1) What purpose does the curriculum seek to attain? 2) What learning experiences will attain these objectives? 3) How can these learning experiences be organized for effective instruction? and 4) How can the effectiveness of the curriculum be evaluated? Within the context of these classic principles, a nursing curriculum must also address the accreditation criteria recognized by the profession and established by its accrediting body, the National League for Nursing (NLN, 1988).

What Purpose Does the Curriculum Seek To Attain?

The purpose of a parish nurse curriculum is to prepare nurses to effectively integrate health and self-care practices with the faith practices of individuals and families within a faith community. This requires a broad base of nursing knowledge and skills along with in-depth knowledge of the spiritual, psychological and physiological aspects of health and illness and the sociological behavior of families and communities. Specifying the role, parish nurse, signifies that this role is not just a registered nurse located in a church, nor a compassionate person in the congregation who serves as a support to those members in crisis, but a professional nurse with advanced knowledge, skills and a faith commitment to promoting the integration of these qualifications in facilitating the health and wholeness of the faith community. Identifying the competencies necessary to attain these goals guides the development of specific objectives the curriculum must accomplish in order for the graduate to implement the role of parish nurse. This is the challenge facing the parish nurse movement today.

What Learning Experiences
Will Attain the Objectives?

The National League for Nursing criteria for the evaluation of curriculum for the master's degree specifies that the curriculum be internally consistent and reflect the philosophy and beliefs of the school (NLN, 1988). This requires that specialty area curricula be consistent with the graduate program as a whole as reflected in a common conceptual framework, terminal objectives and core courses used to develop the specific curricula for all advanced nursing practice specialties. The criteria further specifies that the curriculum: 1) builds on the knowledge and competencies of baccalaureate education in nursing and provides for the attainment of advanced knowledge of nursing and related theories and their application to advanced nursing practice, 2) provides opportunities to identify and participate in nursing research and 3) provides theoretical and learning experiences in the development of leadership, management and teaching skills. These criteria present the consensus of the profession on the process of graduate education and provide the structural framework for building the curriculum, regardless of the specialty.

These criteria imply that students will have an opportunity to practice in a setting where there is an appropriate role model. As a new role is defined and developed there is always lag time before the "ideal" clinical practice settings are developed. Until sufficient numbers of parish nurses are prepared at the advanced nursing practice level, educators are challenged to create appropriate experiences for students.

How Can These Learning Experiences
Be Organized
For Effective Instruction?

This question addresses the conceptual framework for the organization of the curriculum which is essential to ensuring that the educational process proceeds in a logical fashion and that essential knowledge and skills are attained. While the need for using a specific theoretical framework in graduate education has waxed and waned, there is value in using an organizing conceptual framework for a graduate program in order to maintain the internal consistency of the program as specialty area curricula are developed. Several nursing theoretical models exist which can provide the organizing structure to a parish nurse curriculum.

How Can the Effectiveness of the Curriculum Be Evaluated?

The long-term and ultimate effectiveness of the curriculum will be evaluated by a significant positive change in the health of clients (individuals, families, congregations) based on specific parish nurse interventions. Hence, large-scale, longitudinal studies of the health and health behaviors of congregations must be designed and implemented. It will only be as the cost effectiveness of parish nurse interventions, as valued by the congregation, is demonstrated will the parish nurse role take its place on the paid ministry staff of the congregations which must make many fiscal choices.

A Curriculum For Advanced Nursing Practice As A Parish Nurse

At Georgetown University, the parish health nursing specialty is one of the continuing care specialties which currently includes: gerontologic nursing (gerontologic nurse practitioner), adult health nursing, adult oncology and immune deficiency nursing, adult critical care nursing, and primary family health nursing (family nurse practitioner). Clinical specialists/practitioners are prepared to be expert practitioners in an area of practice focused on the continuing care of a specific population, such as older adults; a population with a common health need, such as cancer; or a population in a specific practice location, such as a critical care unit or church. Sufficient didactic and clinical instruction is provided to meet professional certification in the specific specialty areas where certification is available. While there is a strong clinical practice focus, students also have didactic and clinical learning experiences in all the functional roles of the clinical specialist. The clinical specialist is expected to be able to assume leadership positions in the health care system as an expert practitioner, educator, manager, advocate, researcher and consultant. Each student is encouraged to choose learning experiences and elective courses which meet his/her professional goals.

The Graduate Program Organizing Framework

The curriculum is divided into three components. The first component consists of the core graduate program courses which provide essential knowledge and skills to all advanced nursing practice roles; nursing theory and research, and organizational behavior and management. The second component contains courses that are core to the clinical specialist role in the Continuing Care Specialties; clinical specialist role development, advanced pharmacology· and pathophysiology, and concepts in advanced nursing practice. The third component consists of the clinical specialty courses which expand and apply the concepts and knowledge of the core courses to the specific areas of clinical specialization, such as Parish Health Nursing. The program of study is 36 credits, which can be completed in one year of full-time study or three years of part-time study.

The organizing framework for the graduate program is the general systems theory which explains the structures (subsystems), processing (interaction), and goals (outcomes) of systems and the impact they have on and from the supra-systems, such as the health care system. The organizing framework places specific emphasis on the interaction of three primary systems: the client system, the nursing practice system, and the health care delivery system. The structure, process and goal within each system further delineates the framework to assist in the organization of a logical and consistent graduate curriculum which provides the structure for each of the specialty curricula.

Organizing Framework
Graduate Program

	Client System	Nursing Practice	Health Care
Structure	Life Cycle Human Needs Individual/Family Group/Community Culture	Nursing Theories Nursing Science Technologies Ethics Values Roles	Community of Providers Primary/Secondary/ Tertiary Levels of Care Law Ethics
Process	Nursing Process - Assessing - Planning - Intervening - Evaluating	Practice Research Leadership Management Education Consultation	Interdisciplinary Practice Political Process Legislative Process Health Care Economics Administration
Goal	Optimal Health	Advanced Nursing Practice	Effective Health Care Delivery

The elements of the three systems, client system, nursing practice system, and health care system, of the organizing framework are incorporated into both the core courses and the specialty courses.

The client system includes four structural elements: life cycle; human needs; the individual, family, group or community; and culture. Nurses assist the client system toward its goal of optimal health by means of the nursing process; assessing, planning, intervening and evaluating. Optimal health is that state of health desired by the client, given the knowledge, ability, resources and motivation.

The second system of the framework is the nursing practice system which has as its goal advanced nursing practice. The structures essential to achieving this goal are: nursing theories, nursing science, technologies, ethics and values, and roles. The processes of the nursing practice system—practice, research, leadership, management, education and consultation—use the structures to achieve the goal of advanced nursing practice.

The third system, the health care delivery system, has as its goal effective health care delivery. The structures of the health care system are: the community of providers; the primary, secondary, tertiary levels of care; law; and ethics. The processes—interdisciplinary practice, political and legislative processes, health care economics and administration—facilitate the goal achievement of effective health care delivery.

The Parish Health Nursing Curriculum

The Parish Health Nursing specialty began in the fall of 1989 as one of the Continuing Care Specialties. The Continuing Care Specialties provide a core curriculum for preparing clinical nurse specialist/practitioners in the continuing are of adults and families from wellness to death in a variety of settings, such as the church, and for populations with special needs. The expansion of the graduate program to include Parish Health Nursing is a logical extension of the specialty options within the graduate program and is congruent with the school's philosophy. The Continuing Care Specialties stress the wholistic approach to advanced nursing care of individuals and families during various stages of development. The theoretical framework for organizing the specialty curricula under the Continuing Care Specialties is the self-care deficit theory of nursing (Orem, 1982). Health deviation concepts are drawn from nursing diagnoses (NANDA, 1988), medical diagnoses, psychological diagnoses (DSM, 1980), and theological and pastoral care concepts in order to identify content and learning experiences essential to the parish nurse role.

The self-care deficit theory of nursing states that nurses intervene only when the client (individual, family, community) can not achieve their health/wholeness goal, as they define it, due to lack of knowledge, skills, ability or motivation. Self-care needs arise from universal requirements of all humans—air, food, water, elimination, social interaction and solitude, activity and rest, protection from hazards, and normalcy; from developmental requirements; and requirements resulting from physical, psychological, social, and spiritual deviations or dysfunction.

The goal of the parish health nursing specialty is to prepare nurses to promote the optimal health/wholeness of a faith community through the integration of advanced nursing practice knowledge and skills into the worship and faith dimensions of the client. Specific client systems addressed are the individual members, families, groups within the faith community, the faith community as a whole and its outreach ministry. The structure of these client systems are primarily addressed in the Concepts in Advanced Nursing Practice I and II courses and applied in the clinical specialty courses of Parish Health Nursing I and II which are taken concurrently. The assessment of the client's need for educative/supportive, partially compensatory or totally compensatory nursing intervention (Orem, 1982) due to common self-care deficits which arise from the client's inability to meet universal, developmental, and/or health deviation self-care needs is the focus of the client system. Application of specific content and skills relevant to the role of parish nurse occurs in the Parish Health Nursing courses, culminating in the Advanced Practicum in Parish Health Nursing. The goal of the client system is to promote optimal health/wholeness, as defined by the client, individuals, families, and groups, which are the subsystems of the faith community and influence its health/ wholeness goals.

The goal of the Nursing Practice System is parish health nursing practice, with the structures being nursing science, technologies, ethics and values, and roles. Nursing as a science is taught in the Nursing Concepts and Models course and the research sequence, which culminates in a completed research project or thesis, and is applied in the Concepts in Advanced Nursing Practice courses and clinical specialty courses. The theological content is introduced in the advanced concepts course but is expanded as appropriate in the Parish Health Nursing courses and integrated in the seminars and clinical conferences which are co-led by clergy-persons with particular expertise in the seminar's focus. In addition, elective courses may be taken from among the 11 seminaries, representing most denominations, in the Washington Theological Consortium. The technologies empha-sized are those used in health assessment, education, and monitoring of the client's movement toward wholeness. The role components of the clinical specialist/practitioner in par-ish health nursing are explored in the Clinical Specialist Role Development course and applied in the clinical specialty courses. Specific roles emphasized and applied to the parish setting are; expert practitioner, health educator/counselor, case manager, advocate for vulnerable clients, and research-er. Ethical and legal implications of advanced nursing prac-tice in various settings are also analyzed with special attention to autonomy, beneficence, distributive justice and access to care in today's aging society. Students must demonstrate confidence and competence in assuming the independent and collaborative functions within the parish, with other health professionals and with institutions in order to promote the client's health potential.

The health care system in which the parish health nurse practices is formally examined in the Management and

Organizational Behavior course, which is a core course for all graduate students. The concepts and skills developed in this course are an integral part of the clinical practice experience as the organization and behaviors of the faith community and its interface with the health care system is analyzed. Due to the complex social, economic, legal and ethical issues that impact on the clients' ability to achieve their desired health potential, the student must be socialized into the roles of leader and collaborator with numerous healers, recognizing the unique contribution of each. While students focus their clinical practice in the parish setting, they are exposed to the service access, and economic issues of the continuing care of clients from the health promotion in the parish, through community and home health resources, to acute and long-term institutional care, in order to better oversee client care and to mobilize the social support systems within the parish. Experiences in advocating for appropriate, least restrictive environments which foster wholeness exposes the student to the complexity of advanced nursing practice and the need for involvement with informal and formal power structures within and outside of the faith community.

The Georgetown University School of Nursing, Parish Health Nursing curriculum is an example of a curriculum designed to prepare the parish nurse at the advanced nursing practice level and reflects a philosophy of specialized nursing practice and graduate education. Curriculum development is a dynamic process which must respond to the needs of society and to the nursing profession. As the opportunities for direct reimbursement for nursing and case management services provided by clinical nurse specialists begins to be available through federal and state legislation, it is important that the parish nurse role is positioned so as to tap these sources of financial support which will continue to be the greatest constraint on parish nurse practice.

The educational preparation of the parish nurse will be no easier to come to consensus on than has been attaining consensus on the generic preparation of professional nurses which has led to the multiple entry levels; diploma, associate degree, baccalaureate degree, masters degree, or nursing doctorate. Using the advanced nursing practice role of the clinical nurse specialist as a model for charting the future for parish nursing is one approach. It is evident that there must be a cadre of parish nurses prepared at the advanced nursing practice level, a masters degree, in order to be recognized as a legitimate nursing specialty. The advanced nursing practice role of clinical nurse specialist encompasses not only the expert clinical practice function but also the functional roles of educator, manager, advocate and researcher. These roles are essential to the full implementation of the parish nurse role and can only be achieved with formal academic preparation in these functional areas.

Designating the masters level of preparation for the parish nurse does not imply that only those nurses prepared at this level should practice as parish nurses. It is not realistic to expect that sufficient numbers of nurses would seek this advanced preparation nor is it necessary that all parish nurses practice the full scope of the CNS role. Nurses prepared in postgraduate continuing education programs can be very effective in implementing those aspects of the parish nurse role for which they have been prepared. Most important is that those who use the title "parish nurse" have the knowledge and skills to practice within recognized standards of practice and that the client — individual, family, and congregation — understands any limitations of practice due to education and experience.

Reference List

Ericson, E. (1950). Childhood and society. New York: Norton, p. 263.

American Psychiatric Association. (1980). Quick reference to the diagnostic criteria from diagnostic and statistical manual of mental disorders (3rd ed.). Washington, DC: Author.

Kim, M., MacFarland, G. & McLane, A. (1987). Pocket guide to nursing diagnoses (2nd ed.). St. Louis, MO: C.V. Mosby Co.

National League for Nursing. (1988). Criteria for the evaluation of baccalaureate and higher degree programs in nursing. New York: Author.

Orem, D. (1982). Nursing: concepts of practice. New York: McGraw Hill.

Tyler, R. (1970). Basic principles of curriculum and instruction. Chicago: The University of Chicago Press.

Section IV

PARISH NURSING:
A DEVELOPING COLLABORATIVE PRACTICE

14

TEAM MINISTRY IN THE PARISH

Leroy Joesten

Nurses who have had clinical experience in a hospital setting are usually familiar with the multidisciplinary team concept. The parish nurse needs to reflect on this hospital experience of team and translate it into the parish setting. Congregations are needing to expand their thinking about the nature of ministry and the nature of health. Even congregations that agree with the idea that communities of faith can be places of healing (in a wholistic sense) and that the profession of nursing has a legitimate role in the church structure to promote that idea, may not immediately or unquestioningly accept a nurse as a member of the church staff. Though gaining popularity among nurses, congregations and health care institutions, parish nursing is still in its infancy. This chapter explores some of the issues that surround a nurse as she becomes part of a congregational staff.

Team Concept in Health Care

Though there is evidence that a team concept was emerging in health care already at the turn of the century, it was not until after World War II that it experienced its most dramatic expansion. Though the idea of team had flourished for decades in the mental health field, it was not until after World War II when what was commonly accepted in the mental health field made its way into other health care settings as well.

Three factors are often cited as the key contributors to the general acceptance of interdisciplinary teams in health care.

First, after World War II there was a rapid expansion of hospitals and hospital-centered medicine (Lecca & McNeil, 1985). Funds were readily available for capital investments and also a wide array of services that this fertile environment cultivated.

A second factor was the dramatic advance in medical technology. Not only did this phenomenon contribute to specialization among physicians, but it helped create a vast assortment of other health care professionals as well.

A third factor was a broader understanding of health. Individuals became more active in their health care decisions. Meredith McGuire has documented the multiple ways in which many average Americans are using a variety of conventional and unconventional methods in an effort to cure their ills or promote health (McGuire, 1988).

Changes in Health Care Delivery

Even the casual observer is aware of the dramatic shift in health care delivery taking place away from inpatient settings to community-based, outpatient services. The inability of the health care industry itself to keep the costs of health care even with the rate of inflation has resulted in both government and private measures to set limits on reimbursement for health services. As more and more services have gone unreimbursed by government entitlement programs, private insurers or managed care plans, we have witnessed hospital closings, shorter patient stays, cost containment measures and staff shortages.

Again, the reasons for this shift are numerous. For one thing, hi-tech medicine, even though it has considerable glamour, benefits relatively few people in our society.

Granger Westberg's zeal for promoting wholistic health centers and parish nurse programs has been fueled by the fact that a small percentage of the population absorbs most of our health care dollars today.

Second, hi-tech medicine is very expensive. Hospitals often stake their reputations on having the finest state-of-the-art facilities in order to attract the most excellent staffs and an ample number of clients who will benefit from such services.

Third, we know that the most dramatic improvements worldwide within this century in life expectancy and infant mortality are the result of improved sanitation, hygiene, nutrition and the discovery of antibiotics. James Mason, Assistant Secretary for Health, Department of Health and Human Services, summarizes a conclusion of a recent Carter Center for Disease Control consultation by saying that "we can become much healthier people by making more effective use of what we already know about prevention and intervention of disease." (Mason, 1990)

Changes in Congregational Life

Just as there have been major shifts in health care delivery, major changes have also occurred in the church in recent years. One major shift has been greater mobility of congregants. Just as shorter patient stays influence the ways in which hospitals deploy their resources, so the movement of parishioners from one community to another has required churches to develop new techniques in mobilizing resources and getting to know their members.

Shortages of ordained clergy in some denominations have resulted in training programs for laity. The priesthood of all believers is more than a theological concept, it is the very means of survival for many congregations and the only assurance that ministry will continue.

The authors of <u>Megatrends 2000</u> have noted that American baby boomers who rejected organized religion in the 70's are returning to church. However, they may not be returning to the church or denomination of their childhood (Naisbitt and Aburdene, 1990). Interdenominational marriages may also contribute to the ease with which couples or individuals "shop" for a church home.

These issues, along with many churches facing varying degrees of financial concerns, have forced the church to rethink its mission and to find more effective ways to minister to its congregants.

The Churches Response

Religious institutions have long been invested in health care. As we experience a shift in the delivery of health care services, churches are reevaluating their role in caring for the sick, injured and dying. Indeed, many religiously oriented hospitals have been sold to nonsectarian groups. Others have merged with neighboring institutions, while, as stated earlier, others have simply closed or gone bankrupt.

What is the Church's role in health care today? One response has been that congregations, which are community based, have picked up the banner of health promotion from the religiously affiliated hospitals which are more immediately identified with the critically ill. There is a convergence of an emphasis on team ministry within congregations with the shift within health care from acute care settings to community settings. As these forces merge, the nurse is becoming a leading figure. The parish nurse concept is one model where churches can cooperatively work with health care institutions to address the needs of their parishioners.

Team Concept in Congregations

If it has been fairly recent that general health care needs of individuals are shared among many different health professionals, it is even more recent that a team concept of ministry has arisen within congregations. Different disciplines within church structures have been longstanding, including orders of nuns in the Roman Catholic tradition and deaconesses in the Protestant tradition. However, in the past 20 years, more disciplines have become involved in the ministry of the church, i.e., youth minister, ministers of music and Christian education, etc.

Now, more than ever before, congregations of all stripes boast of shared ministry, or as the health setting calls it, "team ministry."

However, what is true in the health setting regarding team is also true in congregational structures, namely that the involvement of a number of professionals (on a staff) does not in itself ensure a team approach.

A basic definition of a team is "a functioning unit, composed of individuals with varied and specialized training, who coordinate their activities to provide services to a client or group of clients." (Durmis & Golin, 1979, p. 3) This definition suggests three features of a team which have relevance for the parish nurse, as well as other members of the congregational team, namely role, goal and organization.

Role

I liken the experience of nurses trying to define or justify their role in the parish setting to that of community ministers who have had to define or justify their role in the medical setting as chaplains. That process has not been an easy one, and there are many who remain unconvinced that clergy have a valid role to play in the health care setting.

It used to be common that chaplains in hospitals were either retired ministers or those who were said to be ineffective in pastoring congregations. Their role was usually defined in very narrow terms which emphasized overtly religious acts, such as administration of sacraments, prayer and use of scripture. Frequently, clergy were thought of as ''in the way'' or as obstacles to primary medical care for patients.

There are two things that I believe help to define one's role. The first is training and the second is expectation. In an effort to gain more respect from other professionals, movements developed within mental health institutions, hospital settings, etc. that gave ministers more indepth, specialized training in the behavioral sciences. Pastoral care as a clinical specialty has its roots as early as the 1920's through the pioneering leadership of Anton Boison and Richard Cabot (Holifield, 1983).

The clinical pastoral education movement did expand the repertoire of helping skills that clergy possessed to complement their appreciation for the rituals and symbols of their faith tradition. As clergy's clinical skills in listening and counseling increased, their role became more blurred with the role of other professionals who not infrequently felt themselves in competition with the chaplain. Chaplains were challenged to define, claim their uniqueness as clergy, evermore pushing them toward those behaviors which were more overtly religious. There remains a tension for chaplains between a narrow, limited focus and a more comprehensive, wholistic understanding of ministry, between the values and practices of their faith tradition and the technologically sophisticated world of hospitals (Holst, 1985, pp. 12-27).

Over the past 20 years, the role of the chaplain in the acute care setting has become much more accepted. The chaplain has become an important member of the multidisciplinary team and the spiritual needs of patients are becoming more recognized and addressed.

I think many nurses who find themselves in congregational staffs are feeling a similar tension in the definition of their role. The traditional role for nurses has been more task oriented. The nurses with whom I work seem attracted to parish nursing because it is not so task oriented. They feel they can be more themselves. Their work is more relational and viewed to be ministry in a way that conventional nursing often is not. As parish nurses, they can more unapologetically give expression to their faith within the context of their work by addressing the whole person. It is true that the parish setting may grant greater liberty to nurses to give expression to their faith and to do those things which in the past were limited to ordained clergy, e.g., prayer, sacraments. But is this what the congregations in general or specific congregants actually expect from their nurse? Often, parish nurses are challenged to claim those skills and abilities for which they are trained and which make them uniquely nurses. This tension continues to exist.

Various approaches to the training of parish nurses are developing across the country. There are formalized advanced degrees, continuing education programs along with institutionally based inservices. In the Lutheran General program, a heavy inservice component has been built into the role. After orientation, the parish nurses come to the hospital twice a month for ongoing educational and support activities. A hospital "faculty" of chaplains, a nurse educator and a family practice physician coordinates these activities. This "faculty" also has the opportunity to model the team approach to the parish nurses, pastors and congregational members.

Along with training, expectations also help define one's role. These expectations are both external and internal. External expectations are those placed on the nurse by other people. Just as patients in a hospital expect certain behaviors from a chaplain because of their experience with clergy in a congregational setting, so persons in a congregation will expect certain things of nurses because of their experience with nurses in a medical setting. Hospital patients may be chagrined if a chaplain doesn't pray with them while a parishioner may be surprised if the parish nurse does offer to pray with them. Just as patients in a hospital may be frustrated if a chaplain focuses more on their feelings than on their religious presuppositions, a parishioner may be disenchanted with a nurse if she doesn't seem knowledgeable about a particular physical condition.

On the one hand, nurses must be able to respond to the specific expectations parishioners might have of a nurse, yet on the other hand, nurses must exceed those expectations in the quest for a more wholistic understanding of the person. It is not unusual for individuals to come to a parish nurse with a presenting physical concern only to find the majority of time spent talking about loneliness, older parents or a troubled marriage.

There are also internal expectations with which parish nurses live. As much as they try to be free of the limits of a traditional understanding of nurse, they frequently seem to be victim's of it. They struggle against the need to be expert or knowledgeable in all phases of health care. Their role as a representative of the church carries with it additional burdens. A nurse may believe that a parishioners' attitudes toward the church will be determined by how well she is able to meet their demands. Not wanting to be an offense to parishioners, the nurse may find it difficult to set limits on the many demands that people make on them. People can be as demanding, unreasonable or manipulative in a congregational environment as they can in a hospital context. Nurses need support in saying "no," in setting limits with congregants on the basis of time, limited capability or availability.

One hour of Lutheran General's bi-monthly time with the nurses is spent openly discussing their feelings, frustrations and struggles with internal and external expectations and how they are affected by them. Specific case presentations by the nurses form part of the foundation for this discussion.

Goal

Inherent in any group of professionals coordinating their activities is the issue of congruence between each person's role and the institution's mission or sense of purpose. Just as all hospitals have an assumed common purpose yet adopt individualized ways of articulating that purpose, so do churches have a common calling yet distinctive ways of expressing their mission. Such definitions of objectives can be a reflection of the church's surrounding community, the makeup of its constituents, its ethnic and theological heritage. Just as congregational members must be aware and feel comfortable with the goals and directions of the church, the parish nurse also needs to have a clear sense of the goals and mission of the church in which she works.

In his book Congregation, the late James Hopewell (1987) identifies four ways in which congregational cultures can be defined, each way implying a different goal or mission. Hopewell refers to these as contextual, mechanistic, organic and symbolic.

Contextualism sees God's saving activity in the world at large. In the 1960's, under the watchful eye of sociologists like Peter Berger and Gibson Winter and spurred by the spirit of ecumenism, congregations reached out to the broader community not to bring in more members but to participate in God's work toward a full creation. The analogy that

Hopewell uses is that of househunting. Many people select the home in which they want to live as much on the basis of the community as on the house itself. People may be more concerned about the school system, transportation, shopping, than the style or architecture of the house. The Church's role in the world is still a central concern for many congregations as they define their life and work today.

In Hopewell's opinion, the appeal of contextual studies waned in the 1970s and was replaced by mechanistic and organic studies of congregations. To follow the househunting analogy, desirability of a house is conditioned by its serviceability. Does a particular house work well? What is the cost to maintain it? This emphasis is best exemplified by the "church growth" movement. Here the goal is growth in size of membership. God's saving activity is seen in individual souls, so that the Church prospers as souls are added to the kingdom as evidenced by the numerical enlargement of the congregation. The congregation as a "machine" is promoted by techniques such as annual reports which collect data about money, membership, and meetings. Whereas the mechanistic approach values homogeneity, the organic approach stresses heterogeneity. Differences are welcomed as people see potential growth in a mixture of values, backgrounds and interests. As an organism, the local church grows not externally but internally. What is it that makes a house a home? It is that difference which helps distinguish the organic approach from the mechanistic one. Whether or not a church is doing what its meant to do is measured by the "closeness" that exists among its members.

Fourth is the symbolic understanding of church culture. The symbolic outlook focuses upon a congregation's identity as revealed through the collective and individual stories of its members. Here the goal is not so much outreach, growth or closeness as the discovery of a particular congregation's views, values and motivations. Hopewell's book elaborates a method for making this discovery.

Yet another approach for understanding the culture of a congregation comes from systems theory. Edwin Friedman (1985) in Generation to Generation sees congregational life as three interlocking family systems, i.e., each family unit within the congregation, the clergyperson's own family and the entire congregation as a family.

These various approaches can be helpful to parish nurses and clergy as they attempt to better understand the culture within the congregation, their goals and mission, and their ways of interacting together.

Organization

The best trained individuals with the noblest of goals will not function as a team unless there is a coordinated effort by the staff and congregational leadership. Teamwork requires an administration that recognizes the unique contribution of each team member while keeping the congregation's goals in proper focus. At least three ingredients are foundational for a healthy administration of team: communication, respect and accountability.

We observe great diversity in communication methodologies among the 16 congregations in Lutheran General's parish nurse program. These differing methods are usually the product of both denominational idiosyncrasies and the leadership style of the congregation's senior minister. The most satisfying communication method for our parish nurses is one where there is ample opportunity for face-to-face conversation with all members of the pastoral staff. Those who conduct staff meetings on a regular basis promote a feeling of shared ministry which reduces each individual's sense of isolation and subsequent uncertainty about his or her role.

Meetings can be a bane or a blessing depending on how the time is orchestrated. Those that seem most appreciated are those that are the congregational team's version of a traditional multidisciplinary team meeting in the hospital setting. Usually conducted on a weekly basis, each staff member has the opportunity to discuss congregants who are ill, going through a personal crisis or pose a particular concern or problem for that staff person. It may range from discussion about who is hospitalized or shut-in to one of suspected elder abuse or neglect, evidence of a strained marital relationship, someone's abuse of alcohol or drugs, or a member's inability to care for him or herself alone anymore.

Experiences, perceptions of the concern and suggestions for follow-up are contributed by all members of the pastoral team. The highest of professional standards regarding confidentiality are demanded. Unlike a hospital staffing, where the team members generally have no other association with the subjects of concern outside of the institution, a congregational staff meeting concerns itself with problems of people who may be well known in a variety of settings by potentially every staff person. Improper discussion of highly personal information outside of the staff meeting can be detrimental to the person being discussed and to the total ministry of the congregation. Where the size of the staff is smaller, this concern is reduced, but by no means eliminated.

Respect for the valid contribution of each staff person seems to be self-understood. The effectiveness with which a staff member is able to relate to a congregant may have less to do with role or responsibility than with personality. Even pastors who theoretically support a nurse being part of the church staff may resent that same nurse's ability to relate to a favored parishioner. At other times, the nurse may be the staff person who is saddled with the parishioner who is the hostile, troublemaker who constantly criticizes the way the church is run. Both responses are indicators of disrespect.

Respect for other team members recognizes both the professional status and the human qualities that people can possess. Close working relationships surface the securities or insecurities people have about either their training or ability to relate meaningfully with others. Nurses, as well as clergy, may well receive negative feedback from peers or congregants regarding the way they responded in a particular situation. An atmosphere which encourages open expression of both negative and positive feedback from peers is one which respects our incompleteness as God's creatures and provides an opportunity for personal and professional growth to occur.

Accountability is also important for effective team work. This includes some formal mechanisms for evaluation of one's efforts. Nurses who have come out of hospital settings are accustomed to routine annual evaluations by their manager. Church structures are often much less formal about the same. Most of the congregations in our program have health committees with representation by several parishioners. These committees help assess health needs of the congregation and give general guidance and support to program activities. Some churches also use the health committee in the evaluation process of the parish nurse.

Since the parish nurses in Lutheran General's program are employees of the hospital, a formal evaluation of the nurse, similar to that of every staff nurse, is requested from the nurse's pastor. We have found varying degrees of comfort with such a formal process. Some have been very imaginative in complementing our basic forms with other evaluative instruments devised by the pastor and health committee. Effective utilization of the evaluation also helps set appropriate and realizable goals for the forthcoming year. Nurses in congregations whose pastors take this exercise seriously feel affirmed in their efforts and very much a part of the church's total ministry.

CONCLUSION

I have enjoyed working with nurses in a hospital setting for many years. For the last four years, as a faculty member in Lutheran General's parish nurse program, I have also had the pleasure of working with nurses who are in a congregational setting. I have been inspired by the idealism with which our nurses have approached their efforts to help congregations achieve greater health, and I have been moved by the seriousness with which they take their own spiritual growth. I feel privileged to be included in their struggles to more fully integrate their faith into their identity as nurses. Parish nursing provides a unique opportunity for such integration to take place. As I have seen some of their idealism of congregations and professional church work fade, I have witnessed a deeper sensitivity in them to their own and other people's humanness. They have come to realize in new and deeper ways that life is a journey which is often marked by unexpected detours and delays. The path to health is not measured by perfection, but by faithfulness and persistence. Health is also measured, not only by what one gains, but by what one surrenders. It is aided by others who are willing to walk with us, without condemnation or prejudice. There is no question that their skills and sensitivity are a rich resource for any congregational staff. The parish nurse concept is still in its infancy. Means of measuring the value of such a program for all who are involved are yet to be developed. With the assistance of a grant from the Kellogg Foundation, Lutheran General is now beginning that challenge. Whatever such studies eventually reveal, I am grateful for the opportunity to work in an innovative way with nurses who are, before anything else, people of conviction and compassion.

Reference List

Durmis, A.J. & Golin, A.K. (1979). The interdisciplinary health care team. Germantown, Maryland: Aspen Systems Corporation.

Friedman, E. (1985). Generation to generation. New York: The Guilford Press.

Holifield, B. (1983). A history of pastoral care in America. Nashville: Abingdon Press.

Holst, L. (Ed.). (1985). Hospital ministry: The role of the chaplain today. New York: Crossroad.

Hopewell, J.F. (1987). Congregation, stories and structures. Philadelphia: Fortress Press.

Lecca, P.J. & McNeil, J.S. (Eds.) (1985). Interdisciplinary team practice, issues and trends. New York: Praeger Publishers.

McGuire, M. (1988). Ritual healing in suburban America. New Brunswick, NJ: Rutgers University Press.

Mason, J.O. (1990). Health care in the U.S. facts and choices. Second Opinion, 13, p. 24.

Naisbitt, J. & Aburdene, P. (1990). Megatrends 2000. New York: William Marrow and Co.

Starr, P. (1982). The social transformation of American medicine. New York: Basic Books.

15

A PERSPECTIVE ON THE PHYSICIAN'S ROLE IN THE DEVELOPING PRACTICE OF PARISH NURSING

Greg Kirschner

*I*t is possible that the title of this chapter elicits two polarized responses during a survey of the table of contents. Perhaps the reader reacts with an "Of course there needs to be physician input into this program!" Alternatively, one might note that "Physicians are always muscling in on programs where they are not necessary, especially when it involves nurses!" This healthy tension has contributed to the enjoyment I have experienced in working with the parish nurse program at Lutheran General Hospital. It is out of my personal experience that this chapter is written, intending to serve as a guide to the potential relationship that a physician may have with a parish nurse program. The primary focus will be the administrative capacity in which a physician may serve such a program, with comment as well on the role of the physician in a community or congregation with a parish nurse. The benefits for the program gained by physician involvement, as well as benefits for those physicians who choose to become involved, will be highlighted. Potential pitfalls for the physician and the parish nurse will also be revealed.

Roles Not Chosen

Before describing the various responsibilities which physicians such as myself may choose to accept in a parish nurse program, I am compelled to outline two roles I have personally chosen not to pursue — or in fact have been offered! The first is that of "Leader/Organizer/Captain of the Ship." The administrative structure of the parish nurse program has clearly called for an interdisciplinary team approach in which the physician is an integral part — but not the central focus, or the key player. This congregationally based, wellness-oriented hybrid of theology and community medicine contrasts sharply with the hospital settings in which most physicians serve in leadership capacities. In fact, placing a physician in the key leadership role in a parish nurse program could subtly point away from a wellness orientation. Thus, I have found myself comfortably serving in an advisory, facilitative capacity — and enjoying it thoroughly! As a family physician, I am accustomed to working in partnership with patients, families and a variety of health care providers in such a team approach.

The second role which I have attempted to avoid is that of "Sole Physician to Needy Parishioners." While the provision of direct hands-on patient care services by a physician is possible, and on occasion appropriate, our parish nurse program functions in a broad medical community, covering a wide geographic range. Those patients requiring physician services may be best treated by physicians of other specialty backgrounds, geographic locales or practice arrangements. While I have enjoyed seeing patients referred through the parish nurse program, I do not view this as a function of my administrative role, but rather as one arising from my role as a community doctor.

Administrative Roles

In the Lutheran General Hospital Parish Nurse Program, family physicians have served administratively in five basic capacities. These include:

1. **Steering committee member** (Holst, 1987 p. 15). Having offered a disclaimer about my personal desire to not be a

central leadership figure, physicians have played an important part in providing direction to the development of our
parish nurse program. Historically, this role was probably
most important in the early years of the program, as the
scope of the program was being determined, and resource
assessment critical. A physician may be particularly able
to provide guidance in the manner in which a community-based program can interrelate with traditional medical
services. Physicians may be particularly aware of sensitive
"political" areas in the medical community at large, and
are often familiar with liability concerns.

Additionally, the presence of a physician on the
steering committee helps provide credibility for those who
believe that physician input is essential to any medical
program. While we hope this type of figurehead representation is diminishing in importance, it can, on occasion, be
critical, not only when negotiating with hospital-based
personnel, but also with parish pastors and wellness
committees.

As in all roles, the exact function will be determined by many factors, including personal desires. Representation on the steering committee does offer the
interested physician opportunity for influencing the direction of the program, as well as dealing with the day-to-day
operations in a limited fashion.

2. **Parish nurse faculty member** (Holst, 1987, p. 14). In this
   capacity, the physician works with the interdisciplinary
   staff to develop appropriate educational opportunities for
   the nurses. This function includes the joint supervision of
   the continuing education program to ensure that program
   goals are being advanced with regard to nurse development.

The practical form of this role at Lutheran General Hospital has included monthly planning meetings with the other faculty members, as well as quarterly meetings with the parish nurses. During the latter, topics of current medical interest to the nurses are addressed, with ample opportunity for questions and answers. These sessions have served not only to update medical knowledge, but as opportunities of mutual encouragement in the philosophy of the parish nurse program as it relates to traditional physician services.

3. **Emergency resource.** Physician availability as an emergency phone resource provides urgent consultative back-up for nurses faced with challenging clinical situations. Having made myself available by phone to nurses for several years, I am struck by the scope and appropriateness of their concerns. I am also impressed by their considerable problem-solving skills, which have often handled the issue properly prior to the call! The nurses have indicated informally that this "back-up" function, while rarely used, is an important provision of the faculty.

4. **Referral resource.** Perhaps the most frequent contact I have had with parish nurses has related to the appropriate choice of "the next step" in a given clinical situation. Nurses may need guidance in recommending the most suitable category of specialty referral. They have requested my opinion regarding diagnostic workups or therapeutic plans for their parishioners.

Quite commonly, the nurses have requested assistance in the identification of physicians who are sensitive to the theology of the parishioner in question. For example, they may be aware of a patient with hypertension in need of a new primary care internist or family physician, but who now wants a physician with a truly wholistic approach. Unfortunately, this type of request is often more difficult to define, with a limited array of possible solutions. The identification of a physician as "wholistic" is highly subjective. The term "wholistic" may even be shunned by physicians who in reality are practicing a highly integrated form of wholistic health care!

Throughout this referral process, a physician in an administrative capacity must be aware of the "political" sensitivities of the medical community. For example, I have attempted to avoid favoritism to my own multispecialty group members, and to offer nurses at least two alternatives for referral, if possible, when requested "for a name."

Rarely, this role, as well as that of emergency resource, has included the urgent provision of hands-on clinical services. As a family physician accustomed to the role of "primary care physician" or "physician of first contact," this function comes naturally. However, in part to avoid accusations of self-serving behavior, and more importantly, to keep the program focused on a community-based, wellness-oriented agenda, I have avoided simply automatically taking each potential referral. I believe this has helped my credibility with the parish nurses, as well as with the members of our hospital's medical staff familiar with the program. I do enjoy patient care, however, and the excitement of caring for this patient population is considerable, as I will discuss later in this chapter.

5. **Resource for educational programming.** The parish nurses are truly experts in seeking out community resources for educational programs in their respective congregations. Physicians have made themselves available as a physician speaker resource if there is a request for such presentations.

I hold a full-time position on the faculty of the Family Practice Residency Program at Lutheran General Hospital, and coordinate the family practice residents' experiences in community medicine. An exciting opportunity has developed to give the residents exposure in community education by linking them up with parishes looking for physician speakers. I have personally supervised residents in the development of such programs, and provided formal feedback on the quality of their presentation. While not all physicians in training would feel comfortable, or be appropriate for the congregational setting, for others it has proven a valuable educational activity. At the same time, our residents have given high-quality presentations in the congregations on topics such as "men's health" and "adult health maintenance." This collaborative relationship thus meets goals for both the parish and the sponsoring hospital.

Potential Pitfalls

The administrative relationship I have described is quite unique among my responsibilities. The fluid, team-oriented approach, while utilized in other settings, takes on a different meaning in a program focused outside the hospital on the activities of congregations and nurses. For physicians involved in such activity, the ability to work closely with nurses and pastors through novel and sometimes challenging ideas requires relinquishing some control, as mentioned in the opening of this chapter.

In addition, the parish nurse program can have a tendency to "fall-out" as an add-on activity/responsibility for the physician. That is, as physicians volunteer their time to work on such a program, there can be a tendency to "leave this commitment to last," as important as it might be personally to the physician. This can be a liability for the parish nurse who may be depending on the physician for the completion of certain tasks in a timely fashion.

A brief word to those physicians working for other employers. It is certainly probable that your employer will hold you accountable for the time you spend working in conjunction with a parish nurse program in an administrative capacity, unless it is entirely on your personal time. This calls for careful attention to the manner in which your involvement in the parish nurse program meets your employer's expectations — that is, how a parish nurse program advances your employer's goals. Our faculty group has come to understand my involvement in the parish nurse program as important to institutional objectives, as a unique referral source and as an avenue of achieving educational goals for the residency. Such a sponsorship is critical for sustaining activity. I periodically update the other faculty on developments in the parish nurse program, and highlight all resident educational opportunities which have resulted from the program.

Role of the Community Physician

I wish to comment on my involvement as a health care provider to patients from congregations with parish nurses. By way of example, consider the case of Mr. and Mrs. D. Referred by a parish nurse, this couple was looking for a new primary care physician, and lived near our office. Mrs. D. first presented for follow-up, and ultimately required relatively minor surgery. Mr. D. initially presented with an acute attack of gouty arthritis. During the ensuing months, I came to know this couple quite well, although there were no explicit conversations regarding their expectations of me, and I had little insight into the extent of their involvement in the local congregation. However, on one occasion I inquired of Mr. D. "how he maintained the obviously positive outlook he had on life." He quickly responded with a clear explanation of the importance of his Christian religious beliefs for "the hope that was within him." It was a remarkable doctor-patient office interaction. It achieved greater significance only a few weeks later when, on Christmas eve, I had to inform him and his wife that he had probable metastatic cancer. During the few remaining days of his life, in a time of rapid deterioration in his health, we were faced with addressing questions of life support, pain management and the uncertainty of the underlying primary cancer site. The previous conversation related to his belief system, coupled with the ongoing support of his parish pastor and parish nurse, opened up our conversations to a level of honesty and openness which was desirable for such serious decisionmaking. His family fully participated, particularly as he became unable. Mr. D. chose to forego life support measures, and died within two weeks. Personnel from my office who chose to attend the funeral services were visibly moved by the deep faith of this family, and the supportive structure of the church community. Nearly three years later, I continue to care for his wife, who has recently again referred another family for care.

The case of Mr. and Mrs. D. represents for me much of the positive work the parish nurse program can do when working with the traditional medical community. Beginning with the referral of a family whose care had "fallen between the cracks" of medicine, the parish nurse facilitated the most appropriate management I could have imagined for a patient with the type of malignancy exhibited by Mr. D. While the outcome of death was not prevented, the manner in which his last days were spent was significantly altered by the presence of a committed parish nurse and parish pastor, working together with the patient's primary physician.

The character of my practice has changed through my involvement with the parish nurse program. Through referrals of patients such as Mr. and Mrs. D., and through subsequent patient-to-patient referrals, a significant percentage of my practice now could be characterized as truly interested in a wholistic approach to their health. That is, these patients are seeking to understand their health as related to the physical, mental and spiritual dimensions of their lives, and appreciate a need to integrate these areas even in the medical care they receive through their family doctor. I have also come to care for a number of parish nurses and parish pastors. I am challenged regularly by patients to explain my own religious beliefs, or my thoughts on such difficult issues as life support measures or abortion. In turn, my ability to inquire sensitively of a patient's spiritual outlook and its relation to their health is improving, albeit slowly. I may urge patients to have their parish nurse check their blood pressure, and refer others to explore the counseling resources through their congregation.

My involvement in the parish nurse program has, to date, been personally and professionally rewarding. Most of all, I have witnessed the tangible benefits the program has had in my own community, with my own patients! Opportunities for physician involvement in parish nurse programs are increasing, and I am sure that new models of physician involvement will be attempted. How could a physician not choose to be involved if asked?

Reference List

Holst, L. (1987). The parish nurse. Chronicle of Pastoral Care, 7(1), Park Ridge, IL.

16

PASTORAL REFLECTIONS

Gerald Nelson

The voice on the other end of the phone said, "Our family needs spiritual comfort and direction. I called your congregation because we have heard you care."

An administrator of a junior high school called and said, "We have a young man who recently moved here. He is finding it difficult to adjust and he is acting out those difficulties. Is it possible for you or someone on your staff to meet this family and see if you can help?"

I recently participated in a panel that had been given the task of defining the unchurched and defining how a congregation can reach out to those without a church home. One of the ways I noted was the importance of being known as a caring community. While we have seen ourselves in that light, it is quite true that five years after the advent of a parish nurse in our congregation, others are more likely to think of us as a parish who cares. Our own people can now quite easily verbalize that their church home is a loving community.

Excerpts from a letter written by one of our members illustrates the image of a caring faith community.

My purpose in writing this letter is to comment for the record the valuable service of Christian care recently given to our mom . . . and to us her children.

Though I was serving as vice-president on the parish council at the time of the parish nurse education and implementation, I was not fully aware of just what this service could mean to a church member.

One day in the midst of feeling inadequate in dealing with issues regarding Mom, and in prayer ("Oh God, what more can I do?") the answer came, "Call Saralea Holstrom" (parish nurse). Saralea heard our story and called Mom the next day and became a dear friend to Marie, and a source of peace and support to us, her children.

We are thankful for Saralea, her services, and who she is as a person. It is my intention that this letter be put on file as recommending the parish nurse as a valuable addition to the Parish Staff . . .

With the addition of a parish nurse to our staff, we have increased significantly our capacity for caregiving. That this is important is dramatized by how few institutions there are that really care. While there are institutions and people who say, "We care," what they care about are such things as our response, our business, or our vote. In most cases, it is unlikely they will care deeply, if at all, if a loved one is ill, or an income is lost, or if a child is struggling with self-esteem, or if substance abuse is destroying life, or if someone is desperately lonely.

Congregations are concerned about such things! They believe there is a power in the community that gathers around the Word to heal and bind up, to comfort and restore.

As our society becomes more and more fragmented, the congregation that seeks to carry out a healing ministry of caregiving is like a bright light in a dark place. We have a marvelous opportunity to bear witness to the love of God.

The parish nurse program can move any congregation to a higher intensity of caregiving for it helps to bridge the gap between concept and mission. Concept says we care. Mission is caring.

Our congregation has grown from 1,400 to over 3,100 baptized persons in the past 15 years. Much of that growth has happened because the congregation is seen as a caring community. All statistics indicate that over 75% of those who join congregations do so because of a friend. If members feel authentic caring in their church home, they will feel positive about sharing that church home with others.

I believe we must be able to link together the message that we are loved by God with the message that His grace frees us to be lovers ourselves. It is in that spirit that I relate that two of the most important decisions in our parish in the last ten years were: 1) to become a fully eucharistic community, and 2) to add a parish nurse to our staff.

The first relates to the message that we are loved by God. By "fully eucharistic" I mean that we include the sacrament of Holy Communion at all four of our weekly worship services.

As the sacrament is shared, there is the powerful message of forgiveness, love and new life. There is the opportunity for every person to be addressed with the Gospel. Then too, as we give the bread, our pastors use the opportunity to touch each person. It might be a gentle touch or a squeeze of the hand. In that touch there is communicated the message of love, that we are there for one another no matter how deep the hurt, worry or concerns of the soul.

The second decision, that of adding a parish nurse to our staff, relates to our being a community in mission. A vital part of our healing mission is being available and competent in dealing with the hurts, needs and concerns of people.

One of the many touching moments connected to the healing aspect of our community occurred when a long-time member of our parish was seen in the sanctuary following worship. He was speaking with our parish nurse. What he said to her was, "I have cancer. I have been told I have only a short time to live."

He had received the eucharist. Now he was articulating the reality of human suffering and need. He was in conversation with someone who could understand the technical terms the medical profession had used to describe his illness. He asked for clarification, but mostly he practiced telling his story. As he told his story to our parish nurse in the sanctuary, he was strengthened by the eucharist message received only moments before, that "because I live you shall live also." And healing, the healing of Christ, was among them, and this beloved member of our congregation was able to add another crucial part to the telling of his story.

Let me lift again the claim I made earlier that the parish nurse program has not only enabled the image of a caring community but has indeed increased dramatically the caring we in fact accomplish.

We stress that the parish nurse is available to our people on Sunday mornings. It is the weekly gathering time of the family. Each Sunday, she is surrounded by those who have discovered that she is a valuable resource, a confidant, an interpreter, an advocate, a source of referrals, a friend, one who can help identify options and sort through them. She is also available at other stated times during the week, but the Sunday coffee hours between services are a key time of availability. Her visible availability lifts the message of the congregation being a caring place, a place of healing, a place that listens to one's needs and concerns.

It is very important to see the parish nurse as a part of the pastoral care team. Such a team might consist of the pastor or pastors on staff, the parish nurse, and lay volunteers. In our parish it is our four pastors, parish nurse and a seminary intern. We meet early each week at a set time and review the parish needs and concerns. This has virtually eliminated those dreadful feelings that come to us when we are reminded that "Joe" came home from the hospital two weeks ago but no one has followed up on his progress or evaluated his needs.

We do follow up much, much better with a parish nurse on staff. One reason for this is that a nurse is a professional healthcare person. Nurses are accustomed to "checking in" on people. When we listen to a nurse in dialogue, we hear a steady pattern of conversation that is designed to draw out an articulation of "how are you doing?"

At each pastoral care staffing, we review those who have received care in the last several months and all who have been brought to our attention since the last time we met. We assess the need for follow-up and decide who will do it. Our parish nurse makes many of the follow-up contacts. Many can be made by phone. Her follow-up is so valuable because a nurse is skilled at assessment, and also because there are often questions of a medical nature.

We are sometimes asked if people accept the ministry of a parish nurse as easily as they receive a pastor's offer of care. The answer is yes. If there is hesitation, it is only prior to their having an opportunity to be helped by her ministry. Any hesitations quickly disappear when they have such issues as an aging parent, counseling relating to AIDS, depression in youth, sexual concerns among the youth, chemical abuse questions, the need for resources such as nursing homes, adult day care and divorce or grief support groups.

While a pastor has a great variety of responsibilities, such as being an administrator, preacher, teacher, worship leader, counselor, fundraiser and leader, the parish nurse is able to be a specialist in the parish in the area of caring. Her focus is solely on caring. She demonstrates this caring through establishing support groups for caregivers, writing articles for the parish newsletter, arranging transportation for those who need outpatient treatment and on and on.

This sense of speciality in caring is captured in a letter written by our parish nurse in which she was explaining her motivation and understanding of the program. She writes:

I heard Granger speak about six years ago and was very interested in his vision of wholistic health care based in the church. At the time, I was working as a Medicare staff nurse in a long-term care facility. My brother's wife has multiple sclerosis and I was caring for her on my day off. Several times I called her church encouraging a friendly visit but this never took place. I felt their life could have been so different if they could have had an advocate in their faith community. I have also seen numerous examples in my nursing experiences of how a patient with faith, a relationship with God and a faith community seemed to recover better from crisis and illness.

Out of her experience she has helped us to realize as a congregation the powerful image we can have as a caring community of faith. We have had a surprising number of re- markable recoveries among the people of our parish. While we do not pretend to understand the mysteries of God, we do understand that love and care can be essential to recovery from illness, injury, grief and crisis of any kind. A caring par- ish can play a vital role in this process and any parish in- creases its caring capacity when they have a care specialist on staff.

I am not saying that pastors are not caring persons. Quite the opposite is true. Pastors have such a wide range of responsibilities that we are seldom able to specialize in any area. When a parish nurse came on our staff, we began a new chapter of caring. We stepped it up. It took on new dimensions we had never known before. In my own heart I have always carried guilt and worry that I was not covering all the bases like I wanted. It was a heaviness that someone was forgotten or neglected, that opportunities were being lost. Once the parish nurse joined the caring team, there was a partner and specialist in caring.

Several years ago, we had a young husband and father seriously injured in an automobile accident. Little hope was given for his survival. His parents, who lived out of state, came immediately to help with the children and to assist his wife in keeping the daily vigil at the hospital.

In the days that followed, our pastoral care team, as we always do, talked together about how we could best give care to this hospitalized, comatose man and his family. Even though the hospital was 45 minutes away, we decided together that we would visit that man and his family every day. Our parish nurse was a part of that schedule. Every fifth day she visited as we did not have a seminary intern at the time. She brought the same same value of presence and prayer as did the pastors. She also brought the added dimension of being able to communicate with that family about medical procedures and concerns. She enabled dialogue and understanding which greatly aided the well being of that patient and his family, and helped them all in the healing process. It was a great day when that man returned to the sanctuary where so many prayers had been said in his behalf. As he embraced me after worship, he said, ''Without the prayers and ministry of this People of God, I wouldn't be here!''And his eyes overflowed with tears of gratitude.

Another dimension of the caring of a parish nurse is in the way in which she draws others into the care arena. Not only does she draw volunteers from the parish who are recruited to do such things as provide transportation for outpatient needs, but she draws all of us into the care arena through our contacts with her. A person who is modeling caregiving is one who gives others inspiration, motivation and examples of how caring enriches life.

Just recently, one of our members died following a brief illness. This person had always been so supportive to me and to the mission of our congregation. How can you not love a man who had been a supportive and articulate member of the stewardship committee for 33 successive years!?

After the funeral service our parish nurse sought me out. She knew how hard his death was for me, not only because one pours one's self out in those times, but because pastors, too, experience loss, even in the midst of the good news of eternal life. She reached out, this parish nurse, and put her arms around me, and all she said was, "Oh pastor." That's all. Her voice and her presence told me she understood. And, for that moment, I rested as a caregiver and received care and love from another. It makes a difference to have sensitive and caring people who league together in ministry, either as volunteers or a part of a staff.

Later, as I reflected on that moment, I was reminded again of how important it is to give to others that sense of how a parish nurse can draw others into the care arena through her contacts with them.

The following diagram is not intended to be interpreted as an organizational model as much as an attempt to share some of the ways caregiving works in our parish. Each of the spokes of the wheel has been initiated after the parish nurse program began or has been revitalized or re-shaped.

A word of explanation about the diagram. My brief comments are for the purpose of explaining the role of the parish nurse in some of these areas rather than a description of the program entity.

Prayer is a vital part of our faith life. We are all supported by the prayers of others. The Prayer Line is an encouragement for supportive prayers as well as intercessory petitions on behalf of those in need. The parish nurse recruits and meets with participants. She is the one who gathers prayer concerns, doing so primarily through a prayer concern box, a form in each bulletin, telephone requests, and members of the pastoral care team.

The Wednesday morning, mid-week devotions are tied to the Prayer Line in that intercessory prayers are offered. The staff gives leadership to these 15 to 20 minute devotions held in the sanctuary. If you were to call the church office during this period of time, you will be greeted by a message that says, "the congregation is at prayer." The parish nurse is a part of these devotions, both as leader and participant. It models that one of the ways we maintain and guard our wholeness is through prayer and worship.

Stephen Ministry and LOGOS are both international programs available to all congregations. Stephen Ministry equips the laity for one on one caring. Our parish nurse relates to this program as a resource and as one who is alert to those in need of this personal caring.

LOGOS is a youth and family ministry. As is true in much of our caring ministries, the emphasis is on enabling persons to develop in all the wholeness God intends. In this sense, we can speak of preventive medicine. LOGOS in our congregation embraces 6th to 12th grade youth and their families with the intent of giving spiritual nurture and direction while building stronger ties to the church family. Our parish nurse serves as a table parent at the weekly meal and in so doing is present as a member of the faith family and available to staff and students as a resource person. By her presence she also experiences, firsthand, family concerns and needs.

Helping Hands is not an unusual group in any congregation, yet we find this deepened in that the parish nurse is often in a good position to assess the need for services the church family can offer, such as child care, meals and transportation.

The Health Committee came into existence in connection with, and support for, the parish nurse program. The committee is focused on keeping a health awareness before the congregation. It needs to be said that our parish nurse is a health educator. She leads adult and youth programs in all aspects of the stewardship of life. Her focus is often on children and youth. She gives leadership to church school units on human sexuality. We have two sessions of Vacation Bible School and she is a part of each of those in her role as health educator.

In all aspects of the parish nurse program, and in our entire ministry of caring, it is our intention to articulate that the care given, the concern expressed, and the wholeness prayed for, is done in the Name of our Lord who moved among the people as one who healed.

In a letter received from one of our members, there were these words about our parish nurse: ". . . tell Saralea that when I get home I'm going to pin angel wings on her. What a marvelous caring person she is . . ."

What I want to emphasize here is that in the many letters we receive the word "caring" is used over and over.

In the year when the stewardship theme of our church was "Signs of God's Gracious Love," one of our members gave a temple talk. He referred to the parish nurse program as one of those signs of gracious love:

> Without the parish nurse program some of us would be poorer in body and spirit. But with it there comes a feeling that God is near — that He comes and loves, that He heals and redeems. My wife and I have had various illnesses that seem to come with the aging process. We have been under the care of our parish nurse ever since this program was begun five years ago. We look forward to her visits, because she comes on behalf of the Church, not only with medical knowledge and skill, but also with compassion and love which are uplifting and sustaining.

Returning to the thought of "angel wings," I am reminded of how after the temptation of Jesus in the wilderness, angels came and ministered to him. I am grateful that God still sends angels to minister to his people. God calls out to all of us to be a part of the mighty group of caregivers, angels, as it were. And especially God calls his congregations to be people who are angels who minister in time of need.